A Victim

Bibe

authorHOUSE®

AuthorHouse™ UK Ltd.
500 Avebury Boulevard
Central Milton Keynes, MK9 2BE
www.authorhouse.co.uk
Phone: 08001974150

First published by AuthorHouse 01/14/2011

ISBN: 978-1-4490-6742-7 (sc)
ISBN: 978-1-4520-5803-0(e)

This book is printed on acid-free paper.

Contents

My Birth

1928 had commenced with a week-long blizzard, the worst of the decade, followed by dull laden skies. The latter part of January arrived draped in tiny glints of frost. The nights were bitterly cold and a thin layer of ice covered the roads. It was on such a night that my mother went into labour with her first child. At about 2 o'clock in the morning, my father rushed from the large Victorian house in Notting Hill, where they rented two rooms, to contact a midwife. There were no National Health Service at that time, and the poor and needy were restricted as to their option on health, or should one say, ill health. For most of them the services of a doctor were beyond their purses. In some cases even a midwife was out of their financial reach; they had to rely on friend or relations experienced in such matters.

Dad was a small man, only 5ft 5ins in height and weighing about 9 stone He had a swarthy and sallow complexion, black hair, deep hooded brown eyes, a strong Roman nose and was often likened to, to his secret delight, the great romantic film idol of the era, Rudolph Valentino. An excitable, highly-strung man, he was prone to bronchial asthma, but otherwise was strong and full of vitality and energy. As he ran in the deserted streets of London, the cold frosty air caught his breath.

Arriving, panting at the midwife's house, he banged agitatedly on the front door. A welcoming light shone almost immediately, an upstairs window opened and a woman obviously used to be summoned at night called, "who's down there." Dad gasped out his name and address with an urgent request that the midwife came at once to attend his wife. She readily agreed, and with great relief, Dad rushed back home to be followed in twenty minutes by the midwife, sitting astride a massive, boneshaker of a bike, her sturdy legs, encased in thick, grey, woollen stocking, pummelling the pedals. With a squeal of the brakes, she deposited her bike against the railings, with strong, sinewy arms. The midwife now erect on her brogue shod feet exuded confidence and trust to all who came within her orbit. Approaching middle age, her greying hair was pushed under her cap and she wore a dark grey nurse's uniform. All in all a person most people would welcome as a friend and confidante.

Any major childbirth complications she encountered were referred to a doctor, or in extreme cases to the local hospital, St Charles in Ladbroke Grove. The hospital had previously been the local workhouse and was unpopular with the elderly, who were terrified to receive treatment there in case they were kept for the rest of their lives. My grandmother had these fears and dreaded going there. Unfortunately she had no choice, and died in there following a hernia operation. The workhouses had served as homes for the poor, destitute and homeless. Conditions inside these Poor Law Institutions were appalling and they were run on the lines of a prison. St Charles Hospital remained grim and depressing, retaining its workhouse image for many years. It was eventually taken over by the NHS, and many years later my youngest son at 14 was taken there after a bike accident, as it was the nearest hospital to his school. It had improved considerably.

The midwife mounted the steps to the front door of the stately Victorian home. The house was dark and gloomy, but the bedroom was well lit with a blazing log fire. The kitchen was across the passage, and my father carried in bowls of hot water, comforting my mother as best he could. In common with many woman of the time she had little knowledge of childbirth. That combined with the lack of anaesthetics made the experience harrowing. Husbands were not allowed to be present at the delivery, but Dad was told she never complained or made a fuss in labour. She remained stoical all her life, a stoicism that I did not inherit and remained quite ashamed of the fuss and noise at my oldest son's birth; and the many weeks which followed it. Fortunately my birth was uncomplicated and my parents sat in the warm room sipping hot tea with their new born, baby daughter.

Grandparents

When my parents, William and Winnie Daniel, first married, my father's mother, Minnie, insisted they shared their spacious house in Blenheim Crescent in Notting Hill. The garden backed onto a tree-lined square, the square consisted of well laid out lawns and a shrubbery benched at regular intervals. At one end were two tennis courts where my father and his younger brother played whenever they could. There was a wooden staircase leading from the top floor straight to the garden. All in all, an ideal house for young people and children. Unfortunately the two women were not compatible and their feuds and mutual dislike lasted until death. It was a source of great unhappiness to my father, who loved his mother deeply, and visited her whenever he could take my brother and me with him.

It was not surprising that they were not compatible as their backgrounds were totally different. My grandmother was a country girl; stately built, strong and wiry, with a dominant nose, deep sunken eyes, firm mouth, set in a sallow heavy face. Her dress was always neat and tidy and usually covered by a big black shawl whatever the weather. On her feet she wore high black laced up boots which she kept well polished. She wore large black hats securely anchored to her head with huge hatpins and adorned with a long boa feather. Her father was a fishmonger and attended a convent school where she learnt the piano, sewing and good housekeeping. Unfortunately the marriage was not good and she was a desperately unhappy woman who sought solace in drink. This combined with her domineering personality did not make for peace and harmony in the home.

My grandmother at one time made friends with a black woman in the neighbourhood who took in washing. My grandfather resented this friendship and forbade her to see her. My grandmother then bought a pony and trap, dressed up in her best finery and bonnet, and drove through the town with her friend sitting next to her. This clearly gained some notoriety because this event was portrayed by a local artist in an oil painting. My father kept this picture until his death, but unfortunately disappeared amongst much of his estate to his partner.

My grandfather was a smallish man with pale blue eyes. He was smart and tidy, wore a silver Hunter, pocket watch in his waistcoat and a black bowler on his head. Like most Victorian fathers he was tyrannical and autocratic and his children were expected to be seen but not heard. He was born in 1859 in Duston, Northampton to a miller. A favourite story of the miller was that he swum the local river in winter, while inebriated for a bet. There were five children of the marriage, three boys and two girls, with a span of twenty years between the oldest and youngest. In effect, there were two separate families. The three oldest closest in age were born in the early years of the marriage. My father and younger brother were the babies and remained constant companions throughout their lives.

They were both good sons; emotionally and financially supportive to their mother. It was a blow to her when my father married at 23. She was by then 61 and probably found it difficult to adjust to a new daughter-in-law; especially to one who was taking away her favourite son and child. The three oldest children had all left home at an early age. The oldest boy was brought up by his grandfather, and his two sisters married young. It was reputed that my Auntie Nellie, married at 15, first time round. She married three times in all, but ironically died a widow having been left on her own for many years. Strangely it was not the baby of the family, Albert, who became the favourite, but my father. This was said to be due to the fact that he was born on the same day that her beloved father died. Also he was practical and technical; even as a small boy and was able to do many jobs about the house.

The family lived in Luton for some time, where my father was born in 1903. His sister, Minnie, was 14 at the time and was given the job of taking "her Bill" out in his pram. Once letting the pram race down a hill with, fortunately, no ill effects to my father. She and Nellie were trained milliners and made beautiful hats. Even when they were old ladies, they remained smart and would never be seen outdoors without a hat, gloves and stockings. Luton had a thriving millinery industry and they were both able to work up into their 70's. All the children inherited their mother's strong facial features, her capacity for hard work, and to a lesser degree, a tendency to depression. When depressed she would sit at the piano, playing the same piece of music, 'A Maiden's Prayer', thumping the keys with great gusto at the crescendos. She was an excellent seamstress and spent hours at her sewing machine. Her zeal extended to dismantling the machine for a thorough service. Never a tolerant women, she could not understand why my mother did not have any love for sewing. Both Minnie and Nellie were well known for their moaning.

When their parents moved with the two youngest boys to London, the older children remained in Luton; the girls by that time being married with their own children. My father used to say with a laugh that he left school at 12; possibly with the move from Luton he was never officially registered at a London school. The official school leaving age then was 14, but there were plenty of cheap labour jobs for boys. Later he became apprenticed to his father's trade of carpentry. They were both skilled craftsmen and made beautiful furniture from woods like oak and mahogany. As a child I had a solid oak cot, high chair, playpen and a magnificent dolls house - all hand made.

My grandfather never retired and died in his late 70's. It wasn't easy to retire then, as there was only a minimal old age pension. By the time my mother joined the family, "The Old Lady", as my father called his mother, was drinking regularly and her sons often had the task of escorting her home. Her presence inside the local could be detected by the sight of her small black mongrel dog sitting woefully outside.

In stark contrast, my mother, who was of slight build, only 6½ stone, with blue-grey eyes and reddish hair, was educated at an exclusive ladies finishing school. It was assumed by the school that the girls would marry wealthy men and were not trained in the basic skills necessary for a working class marriage. Her father owned a boot and shoe shop in Notting Hill, which was highly profitable. He employed a deaf and mute assistant nicknamed "Dummy" who never known by any other name.

My maternal grandmother was slightly older then her husband, quiet and retiring and dowdy. She was not interested in social activities or travelling, but unfortunately her husband did. He was a smart charming man, but not physically strong, afflicted with a weak chest and a clubfoot. The latter was no great problem. Being an expert shoemaker he was able to make his own built-up shoe that disguised his disability to only a slight limp. As a high class shoemaker he had many rich clients. Behind the main shop was an inner sanctum where rows and rows of wooden lasts all labelled with tags were stored. These belonged to, what her father, called his "Toffs clients", who regularly had all types of shoes made. His clients came into the workroom where he measured their feet, made adjustments to the lasts, with pieces of leaving or shaving off pieces of the wood, thus ensuring that their shoes were always a perfect fit. Thus he built up a prime reputation in the area, guaranteeing profitability.

As a relaxation, and to escape the health hazard of the cold foggy London winters, Henry travelled extensively, usually to Australia, taking his daughter and the nursemaid with him. Their second trip to Australia in 1913-14 was a momentous time for my mother, as well as Europe. They travelled to New South Wales. A highlight of the trip was crossing the equator where the sailors would perform a King Neptune ceremony. A number of the crew dressed as King Neptune and dunked other members in the swimming pool. It was noisy and great fun for adults and children alike.

On board the ship was a well known comic call Wee Georgie Wood who took a kindly interest in the solitary young girl of my mother. He was a very small man, almost a midget, who always played the part of a child. The happy times were soon undermined by the developing relationship between her father and the nursemaid. On their arrival in Sydney the nursemaid, probably jealous of her teenage charge, soon became hostile towards her. She was sent to bed early each night, and the books that she loved were taken from her. This insidious animosity was kept well hidden by the nursemaid from her lover and he was unaware of the true position.

On the outbreak of the First World War, the three of them set sail back to England. Sailing in darkness they were intercepted by a German ship, however they were allowed to continue. Tragedy stuck while they were crossing the Equator. As a sufferer of asthma, the heat was had become unbearable for my grandfather who suffered heat apoplexy and died. He was only 39 and his daughter was overwhelmed with grief as the flag draped coffin slipped into the sea. She was only 14 and her mother and brother were miles away in England. The trauma of her father's death remained with her always manifesting in such symptoms as a strong antipathy to the hymn, 'For Those in Peril on the Sea'. It was a sad journey home and not helped by the unwelcome attention of some of the men on board the ship.

Parents

MARY WINIFRED (WIN) & WILLIAM JAMES DANIELS

Back home, some wealthy cousins of her father took charge of Win and she was sent to a boarding school in Tunbridge Wells, spending the school holidays at their home, with their children. Her brother, who was only 16, falsified his age, and enlisted in the army, leaving their poor, retiring mother to cope as best she could.

1918

After enduring four years at boarding school, she decided at 18 to join the Women's Army, the W.R.A.C. It was a short spell of army services as the war finished in 1918.

On her demob she sought and found her mother, who was living in London in dire straits and poverty stricken. Her brother had immigrated to America, and was beginning a life full of contrast, ranging form a speakeasy gangster in the days of prohibition, to what we now call a Born Again Christian, cumulating as an Evangelical Minster. His conversion came after an acquittal on a manslaughter charge, on the death of a customer in the speakeasy. At Bible College he met his future wife, who also became an Evangelical Minister. They had a very happy marriage but unfortunately there were no children.

Attempting to make a home for herself and her mother was not easy, as the characteristics that had driven her husband into the arms of another woman also made life difficult for my mother. Basically 'Little Gran' as we called her to distinguish her from my father's mother, 'Big Gran, was a deeply religious woman, indeed somewhat fanatical who appeared to live on another plain. Her home was a haven for many poor unfortunates, down and outs and the odd prostitute who had over worn her usefulness. Anyone with a hard luck story got her sympathetic ear

My mother managed to find work in an exclusive fashion shop in Regents Street, a position that entailed a smart appearance, which so depleted her small wage that little was left for housekeeping, and the transient lodger. Meanwhile a few streets away lived my father. How they met I did not know as they had little interest in common. Dad loved dancing and spent most of his spare time in the local dance hall. It was a popular pastime and most couples met at the local hop. Then again he liked a drink and a gamble. There were no betting shops and street betting was illegal, but there were street runners who used to warn the bookmaker when the police were approaching, adding further excitement to the gamble. My mother neither liked dancing or drinking.

1927

However they met and married, whilst she was 27 and my father 23. They were an ill-suited couple, Mum prudish and antisocial and Dad gregarious and socially active.

After the problems of early married life with the in-laws they moved to the large family house where I was born, which had seen better days with servant quarters in the basements, the property was beginning a decline that lasted until the property boom of the 70's. Now the area has regained the opulence that it enjoyed at the end of the last century, due to its close proximity too the city, nearness to the TV studios and the advert of Yuppie. The characteristics of the Victorian architecture have been carefully preserved and enhance add to the splendour of the area.

But Notting Hill has two faces and in my childhood there were districts as explosive and as violent as today, where the police were forced to patrol in pairs. There was a great deal of poverty, partially caused by the aftermath of the General Strike of 1926. Tuberculosis was not uncommon, particularly among the working class mothers who deprived themselves of food in order to feed their husband and children. The winters were hard especially for some children who were short of warm clothing and sturdy shoes and the elderly, who queued with buckets and spades for cheap coal slack in the merchant's yard.

There next move, still within the district, was to a house opposite a convent, whose outstanding feature was a most beautiful chapel, ornately styled, vivid stain glass windows, lovely chiselled statues and religious objects which were highlighted by rose colour, wooden floor blocks, polished to an enamel like finish and gleaming, wooden pews. Just inside the chapel, by the door, was a small, manually operated organ that required the services of a strong arm to pump the bellows. It was a busy working community and the nuns spent a great deal of their time administering to the poor and needy, which abounded in the vicinity of the convent. Although poor we were fairly comfortable, as being a skilled carpenter, Dad always received a steady income and we kept warm with blazing log fires. Even so we were grateful to receive the odd bowl of dripping that an Irish nun sometimes left on the kitchen table. My grandfather and father were skilled carpenters working for the same firm in Notting Hill. My grandfather helped to build the chapel and later my father did the maintenance work

My parents built up a rapport with the nun that led to their conversion to Roman Catholicism, when I was nearly two. My father became and remained a devout Catholic all his life but my mother did not accept some teachings of the church , notably on birth control, but she stayed a Catholic all her life and received the Last Sacraments in Hospital

Childhood

1930

Shortly afterwards my brother Bill was born the only catholic by birth, into the family. He was called William after his father and grandfather, and Joseph after Sister Josephine the nun.

We lived opposite a large and rambling convent which needed constant repairs of a minor nature that my father undertook, with great willingness and gusto. The local church St Francis of Assisi, also commandeered much of father's time with similar make do and mend jobs. Being within the same area as the convent, it was a poor church and the priests were as badly off their parishioners. Now the old lock up shops have been transformed into mews type, upmarket houses.

My mother never took to Catholicism in the same way and embraced many religions, including spiritualism, during her lifetime, but finally she died a catholic. She would not allow my brother or me to attend the local catholic, junior school, her main aversion being not the religion as such, but the apparent blasphemy and swearing rife amongst the children. This non-attendance meant we had catechism lessons at the convent.

1938

The reverend mother was rather deaf and had a large ear trumpet, which caused great amusement amongst us children as we all had to shout into it, to make her hear us. Some of the more timid approached this ordeal with some trepidation especially as she was apt to shout "speak up, speak up". For all this she was a very kindly soul, who loved children and she and the nuns put on lovely Christmas parties for us, where there were games, such as 'Bow Bells' with plenty of nice prizes. Each child received a present and there were always plenty of cake jellies, fruit etc, which were all too rare luxuries in those days.

When I was about eight years of age we moved somewhat upmarket to Shepherds Bush and joined the local school just around the corner where we both did well, but Bill had health problems which Mum exaggerated somewhat by making him wear Thermogene next to his chest. It had a powerful smell and the teachers always fought a losing battle with my mother, resorted to questioning me as to why my brother had to wear the Thermogene constantly. However with a father and grandfather with chest problems, she did well to keep him from serious illness until fourteen and he developed pneumonia, a result of going out on a very cold night to an air raid shelter during the raids.

Dad was very fond of swimming, and along with Albert spent much of his childhood leisure time at Lancaster Road Baths, which common to a lot of baths had a spectator's gallery along both sides and the high balcony made for some spectacular diving, although this was strictly illegal but difficult to enforce. Dad taught Bill and me how to swim, but Bill being prone to chest problems was not unenthusiastic once he had mastered the art enough to be unafraid of water. On the other hand I devolved a keen interest in the sport and when we moved to the Shepherds Bush joined the Hammersmith Ladies swimming club based at Limegrove Baths. The Prudential had a lively swimming club that took part in many galas and an annual river race at Walton on Thames, and we practised in the lunchtime at the local baths, Ironmonger Row.

1939-45 WAR AND SCHOOL

A few years before the outbreak of war in 1939, my father luckily won a share of the Irish Sweepstake Lottery. The amount was not large, but sufficient to put a deposit on a house in the same district. It had a small garden, a great luxury among the poor and we were all so happy, especially as Dad brought home a lovely puppy dog.

At eleven I was successful in gaining a place at the local girl's grammar school, the Godolphin and Latymer, which was and still is renowned for academic achievement. It was now 1939 and talk of war was rife so that by August evacuation of the children to the country was in full swing. Together with Mum we were issued with gas masks and put on a train to Somerset. A large party of evacuee children plus a few Mums were assembled in the Church Hall in Frome and from there we were allocated to billets.

The summer of 1939 was glorious, with long, sunny days as we walked and played in the Somerset countryside. It was paradise for most of the evacuated children, many of who lived in poverty and slum conditions, in dirty, overcrowded houses and had never seen large, open areas of fields, with the sheep and cows grazing. The farthest some had been was a day outing by charabanc to Southend where they paddled in the mud and ate chips and ice cream on the sea front. Not all the evacuees were happy. There was a small band of young mums with small children and a few pregnant women. Away from their husbands and homes they were desperately unhappy and met in cafes to chat and discus their problems.

1939 SOMERSET

At eleven I had not come into contact with the suffering and problems of unwanted pregnancies, but being often in my mother's company, I found myself listening to distraught woman, who found they were pregnant and had no way of keeping another baby. Some were desperate enough to seek ways of terminating the pregnancy, illegal at that time and resorted to the aid of back street abortionist, often putting their own health at great risk. My mother, terrified of childbirth had earlier resorted to the then newly open clinics of Dr Marie Stopes, the early pioneer of woman's birth control. Such clinics operated in virtual secrecy and were not considered respectable.

The halcyon days of summer passed quickly, and it was soon early September. Few children knew why they had been evacuated and it came as quite as shock on Saturday, as we sat in the packed church, when a sad looking priest came in and announced that war had been declared between England and Germany. To our dismay, Mum immediately burst into tears.

As my school was evacuated to Newbury I joined the local high school in Frome My

It was a good school, of high academic standings and I enjoyed tackling the new advanced subjects, but I wandered by chance one day into the laundry and found it staffed by young, orphan girls, either physically or mentally disabled. They wore drab, shapeless uniforms, standing at large sinks and using scrubbing boards to clean the clothes in the steam filled room. At eleven I was beginning to develop a social conscience and I was struck by the vast contrast between the laundry girls and the young ladies educated at the convent. But with no welfare state and a school leaving age of fourteen, the poor, unfortunate girls were probably happy to have a safe home and job.

My mother when she saw the laundry room had words with the Mother Superior and took me away from the school and I entered the local girls high school .

Our billet was a farmhouse type of cottage, with an extensive garden mainly turned over to vegetable. The occupants were two bachelor brothers in their mid forties, who lived together for convenience and cheapness rather then compatibility. They welcomed mother to their home as they had frequent spells of not speaking to one another and she became a useful go between. Before her arrival they were in the habit of talking to each other through a mutual pet parrot, a large, green bird that sat on a perch in the front room. A voluble bird, he was as perverse as his owners. Another occupant of the house was a large Persian cat who always slept in the best armchair.

It wasn't long before my mother was cooking them huge meals with a vast assortment of vegetables from their garden. She did not mind, as my father was able to visit most weekends from London, travelling on a milk lorry in the early hours of the morning. Although normally fond of animals, for some reason maybe due to tiredness due to travelling, Dad found the cat and parrot very irritating. When the brothers were not about he shooed the cat off the chair, using a swear word which the parrot soon picked up. This caused my mother some anxiety and the cat shot off the chair as soon as it saw Dad.

The milk lorry driver was a friend of Dad's, and transported milk from Somerset to London every weekend. Dad always had friends in very useful occupants. As well as bringing him down to Somerset, he occasionally took us back to London. It was a bit uncomfortable for the three of us as we were squeezed in the passenger seat of the high cabin, but more so for me as I suffered from the win discomforts of travel sickness and a weak bladder and I found any long journey quite a nightmare. Unfortunately my mother was not over sympathetic, probably because she felt it would be stretching the lorry driver's generosity too far to expect him to keep stopping. As a result I developed an aversion to travelling which lasted until I learnt to drive and could stop whenever I felt the need.

1940 SHEPHERDS BUSH

There were very little sign of war, as London was quiet, as the Spitfires and Hurricanes kept the German bombers away from the City. We were all getting fed up with the commuting and I in particular hated country life, so Mum decided to return home. It was not a good decision as soon after the

Germans launched a new weapon, the doodlebug. This was a monstrous flying bomb with characteristics flames coming from the tail ends. When the bomb was ready to fall the engine cut off and that was the time to pray it didn't land in the immediate vicinity, although sadly aware wherever it fell someone would be killed. They were harrowing times, and Bill and I spent many hours in air raid shelters during the day, wondering if our parents had escaped the bomb at work.

The months went by and there was remarkably little activity on the war front at either home or abroad and we returned to London. It was the lull before the storm and soon the bombing started in earnest. In our back garden, Dad assembled an Anderson shelter, a dome like structured of corrugated iron, dug well in the ground with a concrete and brick base. We spent a few nights in it, but it was cold, uncomfortable and not particularly secure. So we went back to sleeping outdoors, but one night my mother, who always received strong premonitions of danger, insisted that we slept in the air raid shelter some 200 yards away. These shelters were purpose built, brick buildings, with slatted benches that could be used as benches as beds and subdued electric lights on the wall. Each one served several streets and there was a cheerful, community spirit among the people. As we made our way home and walked down our road, we started to kick stones and rubble not realising it was from our house which had been practically demolished by an oil bomb. Luckily our dog Spotty survived, by sheltering under an oak table, his only injury being a burnt nose. We were all taken into a rest home, which was run by the local Mission Church, similar to the Salvation Army. A number of camp beds had been set up in the large hall and we were given food and clothes. It was only a temporary home and eventually we were placed in a flat in Peabody Buildings, Hammersmith. It was a large complex with blocks of flats facing a square inside and the main roads outside. Immediately opposite the flats in Fulham Palace Road, was a Catholic church, St Augustine's, which was run by an Irish order. The parishioners were mainly Irish and on Sunday it was quite common to see a large crowd of men, just outside the main door who made a rush to the local, across the road, when Mass was over. Most of them worked in the building trade and lived in digs, sending money home to their families in Ireland. They were lonely and often unhappy. Ireland was not at war and the men were not conscripted, although many Irishmen did volunteer for active service.

The bombing continued and we spent many nights sitting in a downstairs flat with other families. We soon learnt to distinguish the throb of German bombers, which was soon followed by the roar of the Big Bertha guns situated nearby on Wormwood Scrubs. Sometimes we stood at the entrance to the flats, watching the searchlights and the flashes of guns. Occasionally we were caught out in the streets in an air raid and on a cold, foggy night it could be a nightmare. The fogs then were "pea soupers" and you couldn't see a hand in front of you. One such night a bomb fell near us, as we were huddled in the doorway of a building. It landed on a convent, killing nearly all the occupants, who were sheltering the basement. They were nerve-wracking times, which left its scars in me, with a tendency to recurring anxieties states in periods of stress. During the day we attended various education centre s as most schools were evacuated. The schoolwork consisted of lengthy essays prepared at home and marked at the centres. For the second time my mother had a premonition of danger, feeling that se could no longer sleep in the flat, she took Bill and I to the nearest tube station. The tube stations acted as good air raid shelters. They were deep and secure, with the bonus of being beautifully warm. The people who sheltered in the tube took along little bundles of bedding and settled down to sleep, when the last train went through at midnight. They were awoken by the first tube roaring through at around six am and made their way back up the escalators to the outside world.

There was a grand, community spirit and people slept side by side with not a sign of any crime such as theft or sexual abuse, which today seems almost impossible to believe. There was however a terrible accident in Bethnal green tube station, where people fled to escape the bombing and became crushed on the escalators

As my father suffered with asthma, he was exempt from National Service, but joined the local A.R.P, an organisation made up f volunteers who helped the victims of air raids often digging for, hours in the rubble of bombed building, looking for trapped people. On his very first call of duty he was sent to his own flats that had been hit by a landmine.

On our return home from the Tube we met a scene of chaos and devastation. The mine had the block next to ours, killing several people. Our flat was badly damaged and Mum was frantic until she found that my father was safe. We all ended up in another rest centre in a local church, where we stayed for a few days until the flat was ready to be occupied. During our stay the Germans launched a new weapon, the V2 rocket and one landed near us with a deafening ban   T

1942 NEWBURY

Shattered by the experience of being bombed out for the second time, Mum evacuated us again, this time to Newbury, where the Godolphin@ Latymer shared the local girls' grammar school. There we were billeted in a farmhouse with several other London families, mainly from the East End. The farm itself was neglected due to the absence of young men in the army, but two land army girls relieved the labour shortage in the time; conscripted girls, who worked on the land instead of the services. There were some handsome peacocks, which roamed freely at the back of the farm, noisily displaying their beautiful feathers, but visitors to the farm were often disappointed, as the birds seemed to know when there were strangers around.

The old farmer kept cages of ferrets, which he used to catch the many rats that ran about the farm sheds, often venturing to the farmhouse. The farm sheds were dirty and neglected with thick, mud sludge on the ground, which don't bother the children who were fascinated by the ferrets and the old horses that pulled cartloads of mangle morsels, which we fed to the cows.

Dad visited us most weekends and occasionally we travelled back to London on a large double Decker Thames Valleys bus. It was a long journey and as always I was badly affected by travel sickness, my anxiety even extending itself to the dog and he tried in desperation to get off the bus, once succeeding on a busy terminal at Maidstone and we helped up the bus as we chased through the streets after him.

Transport into Newbury was difficult and occasionally we walked it with unfortunate results in my case as I had a nail in the heel of my shoe that dug into my foot, causing a badly poisoned foot. Dad came to the rescue and brought two second hand bikes and taught us to ride them in the rhododendron-lined lanes, near the farm. With some problems I eventually mastered the art of staying on the saddle and together Bill and I started to cycle to school in Newbury every day.

My brother by this time had won a scholarship and was given a place in the local boy grammar school. It was a prestigious school, where the masters wore their caps and gowns and discipline was extremely strict. There was no approved fraternization between the boys and girls grammar schools, but there were liaisons sometimes with tragic results as when a boy committed suicide, supposedly because his girlfriend was pregnant. As the boys were kept distanced from us, they became figures of fantasy and romance and most of us developed heavy crushes, usually on the same boys – the tall, good looking, athletic types.

There were more problems with the girl's school as we shared the building. The local girls used the school in the morning and we had it in the afternoon. Unfortunately there was hostility between the two schools. The London girls had more freedom as they were away from home. They were also lonely and dated the American air force men who were stationed on Greenham Common. The local people frowned upon their behaviour and there was plenty of gossip, mainly exaggerated. The Americans had a black unit and the men were subject to fierce racism and prejudice, which extended to the girls they dated, among them some of the London girls. Another group of girls who received prejudice were the Jewish. They seem to have a great problem in their billets and were continually moving. Bill and I were fortunate having our mother with us, but life must have been difficult for her as we only had one room on the farm in which we ate and cooked using a small primus stove. Most food was rationed and in short supply, particularly meat but occasionally Mum was able to get the odd rabbit and once a hare, which she attempted to cook in a large saucepan perched precariously on top of the primus stove.

Resigning herself to a long stay in Newbury, my mother took a job at the Gas Works, who were short on manpower as the young men were serving in the armed forces. It was her first job since her marriage, as it was the usual practise or married woman to stay at home. The Civil Service and Banks and Insurances companies did not employ married women and the only jobs available were very poorly paid, such as shop assistants.

The work at the Gas Works was hard and Mum was not suitable for heavy manual work; dressed in a navy boil suit and a cap over her hair, she preserved, but the coal dust gave her eczema of the neck and then irritated her lungs, giving her pleurisy. The pain in her chest was severe but after a short spell at home, she returned to work and eventually came to enjoy her new social contacts and the extras that her wages paid for.

When the farm changed hand he had to look for another accommodation and was fortunate to find a little cottage just past the Berkshire/Hampshire borders. There was no water, electricity or gas laid on in the cottage. Our drinking water came from a tap in the front garden and at the bottom of the long back garden was a shed with a chemical closet. It was quite frightening and uncomfortable to visit the toilet in the dark and cold. There was a system of sewage lorries, which changed the closets periodically. An unreliable acetylene lamp provided the lighting. It was a dangerous contraption and one night, when fortunately Dad was on a visit, exploded in Mum's face causing temporary blindness. These primitive conditions were common in small villages and even in London at that time many houses were without baths. However there was a large, black, iron coal range that was excellent for cooking and also kept the house warm. It was a mammoth job to clean the stove using a special black polish, but was well worth the effort to see the gleaming black set off by the brass handles.

There was only one shop in the village and that was a fair walk away from the cottage. Heavy snowfall in the winter often meant house bound isolation which was only relieved by large snow drifters, which cleared the country lanes. To get to school we had a long cycle ride into Newbury, albeit through beautiful scenery as we crossed the borderline between the counties. There were plenty of snakes lurking in the fern bordering the path. They were mostly grass snakes, but due to their size were most frightening to seem them than their more dangerous, smaller cousins the adders. There was no social life for us in the country as all our friends were in town and we were too young to visit the local pub. An occasional highlight was a visit to a race meeting at Newbury racecourse. Mum had managed to get a job in one of the numerous bars at the course and sometimes we were allowed in free through a side gate into Tatterstalls. Dad loved gambling and it was all exciting and enjoyable and the thrill of a race meeting always remains with me. As the bombing of London had slowed down and we were tiring of country life, particularly in the winter when we could be snowed up for days, my mother decided to return home to Hammersmith.

1944 HAMMERSMITH

Mum had enjoyed the financial independence she got from working in Newbury and soon found herself as a wage clerk in the General Electric Company (Osrams) in Hammersmith, which was engaged in the war effort. It was a job she thoroughly enjoyed; the work was interesting, she made friends and joined the social activities such as whist. She took my brother and me along with her to the whist drives, which were held in the basement for safety reasons. It was whitewashed with metal walls and ceiling and we felt reasonably safe when the sirens alerted us to an air raid, which was fairly frequent. It was a good social occasion although my brother was a remarkable slow cards player and irritated many of the players, who complained about him as they changed tables. As some whist players can be notoriously tetchy, I used to disclaim any relationship with him.

My school had partially returned to London and I made two good friends, both shopkeepers' daughters. One was very talented at art and won a scholarship to the Slade School of Art, but unfortunately became pregnant at eighteen and married her boyfriend, a dance band drummer, which finished her art career. My brother joined the Upper Latymer and was doing very well there, but there were air raids day and night and we went back to sleeping in the tube station. Unfortunately my brother went out one night with bronchitis and as a result of the cold night air and stuffy conditions in the tube, developed double pneumonia.

It was a difficult time; my mother was afraid of the raids but had to stay at home to nurse my brother. He was very ill and my mother called in a doctor. He charged 7/6d and gave Bill a new drug M&B. The drug had been used successfully on Winston Churchill and was the beginning of the antibiotic range of drugs. Bill recovered slowly, helped by a young Irish priest who brought oranges from Ireland.

There were two young Irish curates in the church, with very contrasting colouring. One was of fair complexion, with blond, curly hair and the other with black hair and dark skin. They were always happy and loving, although the parish priest was a ferocious man, who ruled his congregation and his curates with a rod of iron. He had a powerful voice with a pronounced Irish accent, and his sermons were full of fire and brimstone, accentuated by heavy thumps of his fist on the pulpit, which caused those parishioners who dropped off during the sermon to shoot off their seats. However the young priest persuaded him to open a youth club and asked my parents if Bill and I could join. Predictably Mum was not keen on the idea, but eventually allowed us to join, with the admonishment that we did not neglect our schoolwork. It was the church intentions that young people met fellow Catholics and married within their religion. In those days to marry outside the faith could result in excommunication. There was a heavy emphasis on sexual morality, with sex being regarded as an earthly passion that had to be strictly controlled even to the extent that married people were asked to abstain as a penance during Lent.

The two young curates were good-looking men and most of the girls had a crush on them, but always kept them at a distance, respecting their celibacy. We were all celibate anyway, as men expected their wives to be virgins when they married. The reverse was not true, so there must have been some promiscuous women around somewhere. Somehow neither of us took to the church youth club. We were serious, academic children, obviously late developers who were not ready for boy girl relationships. In addition we had considerable school commitments of homework.

Examination time came round, and we sat the public examinations under extremely difficult conditions. It was impossible to study with air raids during the day and sleeping in the tube at night. I remember sitting on a blanket, on the platform reading Virgil's Ænead in preparation for my Latin exam. Some of the girls were in much worse positions, having suffered bereavements and injuries in the raids. However I obtained the London Matriculation Certificate, having passed the required number of subjects were credits. Then I made a big mistake and went on to higher education, taking Physics, Chemistry and Zoology. The subjects were too difficult for me and I struggled badly with them.

Although in our late teens we were treated as children. With clothes on rations, our uniform was shabby, darned and the skirts got shorter and shorter as we grew. In winter we had to wear a navy, velour hats, and a panama hat in the summer, and were severely reprimanded if we were caught not wearing our hats outside the school. The current hairstyles were high and bouffant, often with a blond streak in front and the hats sat perilously on the back of the head. Nylon stockings had just about come onto the market, but we wore heavy lisle, which were usually more darn on the heel then stockings. Obviously make up and jewellery was not allowed and it was quite incongruous to see the older girls escorted by their boyfriends, some of them army officers, to the school. One of the girls father worked at the Windmill Theatre, a striptease show that had the reputation of never losing a night's performance during all through the Blitz. She was a striking looking girl, quite sophisticated, who spoke with an insolent drawl that terrified the teachers. They were all single and found it difficult to relate only the most academic of the girls. One unfortunate girl passed around the class a book on birth control, which was confiscated and she was expelled.

In the school holidays we stayed under canvas in the country, picking strawberries, fruit and helping with the harvest as there was still a labour shortage. It was great fun but the country still did not suit me and while on a fruit picking trip, my foot became badly poisoned.

Although on a school party it was still rare to consult a doctor and the top of my foot had turned black before a decision was made to get expert advice. However I was fortunate in one sense, as the swelling burst by the time the doctor had examined it, so lancing was unnecessary to my great relief. Once the swelling burst, the pain eased, but I spent the rest of the trip languishing on a camp bed, while the rest of the girls were enjoying a fairly good time. When the time came to return home I had to be carried onto the train. Mum got quite a shock when she met me at the station in London, although I had previously poisoned a foot while in Newbury, that time on the heel.

Another, later trip was less traumatic for me and rather more fun as in its midst we celebrated VJ Day, a happy occasion at that time, but it brought sorrow when it was realised that an atomic bomb had been dropped on Hiroshima, which prompted the Japanese surrender. This first use of the atomic bomb caused a stir around the world, although future repercussions were not realised, but undoubtedly it hastened the end of European hostilities, as within a year after Hiroshima the war was over.

1947-1954 The Prudential

I was 18 and still at school, but failed my Higher School Certificate (A levels as they are now called) and after some family discussion I left school for a completely new world – my first job, The Prudential in Chancery Lane.

With excitement and trepidation I set out to catch the tube to Chancery I was requiring clerical assistants. I applied and was granted an interview, which I attended along with my mother. The Pru sent my acceptance letter in another applications letter and fortunately she sent it to me.

In 1947 clothes were still rationed, but I started my first day in a conservative skirt and blouse. Dress was quite important in those days and all women had to wear stockings and respectable attire. For the first time I wore a little make up. Going by train to Holborn ,I changed at Chancery Lane. Just by the station was the large, sombre, red brick insurance building, which was to be my second home for the next seven years.

After reporting to the personnel office I was shown into a large open plan office, complete, to my surprise with an all male staff, most of whom I learnt had recently being demobbed from the armed service. A good many were wearing demob suits like a kind of uniform; grey, brown or blue and ill fitting for the lower ranks; the same colours but better fitting with a few extra for the officers. Music Hall comedians had a field day with demob suit jokes and sketches and eventually most of the men had donated them to the local jumble sales.

Some of the staff I learned later had held high ranking positions, but most had been junior officers and the latter found it more difficult to adjust as they had lead exciting and dangerous lives for five or six years, which came a far cry away from drab, mundane clerical duties. The crunch came at lunchtime when they had adjured to the local pub, drank, swapped yarns, became merry, sometimes even truculent relieving their wartime escapades. In the course of time I was inevitability inveigled into joining the odd session and in what seemed like no time at all I was a familiar visitor to most of the local pubs and could generally have been seen on one or other, exchanging good humoured nature banter with fellow workers. Schooldays have become past memories but I had not yet become emotionally involved with any of the men.

My social life evolved mainly around the Young Conservatives, which I had joined. This made rather unique with my father being rank labour, my brother liberal and my mother an ardent Conservative, which led to heated arguments during election time.

I was in a clique of eight, four boys and four girls, emotionally uncommitted but all jolly good friends, so that be it at the Proms, 'Gods' in the London theatres, local hops or day trips we all had a partner. As well as these social activities, the Prudential had a large sport complex at Chiswick by the Thames, with a clubhouse, dance hall, tennis courts and I joined in many of the activities. I was even inveigled into joining the hockey team, a game I thoroughly disliked at school due to the fact we had to play in all weathers wearing only a skimpy uniform while the teacher was dressed in fur coats and boots. As in the past the cold winter got me down and I gave up the hockey team and turned for exercise to my first love, swimming.

At 19 I took my first trip abroad to Paris, along with a small group from the Red Cross. France, like England, was still suffering from various shortages, and for some reason, which I cannot remember there was little milk about. We visited all the well-known places, such as Versailles, the Eiffel Tower and we were taken to the Folie Berges where we stood at the back and were pestered by amorous Frenchmen. Although we had heard of such behaviour, few of us had experienced it, but accepted it as part of the Paris legend. Our party stayed at the City University where we coped with the unaccustomed food and went sightseeing using the Metro. It was a wonderful experience and I revisited .Paris several times before I Married

1949 My Brother, Bill

The next five years were happy and memories of the bombing and evacuation receded from my mind. It was during this period that Bill went to university in Dublin and sadly developed diabetes at twenty. His weight dropped to six stone and he never fully recovered his health but remained reasonably cheerful. By this time we had moved from Peabody Buildings to a house in Rivercourt Road Hammersmith, which we shared with a widow and her small daughter.

As the name implied the river Thames flowed at the bottom of the road and Bill and I often walked along the river path from Hammersmith to Barnes, crossing both bridges, accompanied by our old dog. Sometimes at Chiswick the water overflowed on to the path, which added to the excitement of the walk. The dog also enjoyed these walks but had an irritating habit of rolling on dead fish that had been left on the path as the river receded. The smell was appalling and he had to be thoroughly washed when we got home.

Politically my father, brother and I, had different affiliations. My father was a fervent Labour supporter, my brother was a Liberal and took an active interest in local politics and Mum and I were Conservatives .Election time became battle time and I was glad when it was over

Bill and I were exceptionally close for brother and sister but after we both married we lived miles apart and never regained the deep friendship we had as children. When he dropped dead at forty in a busy road in Stoke on Trent, I had not seen him for several years. He was kind and gentle and suffered the affliction of near blindness - the effects of severe diabetes – with resigned acceptance. Due also to his illness, he and his wife were not able to have a family. They could not adopt a child, as Bill was a Roman Catholic and Millie agnostic. Neither the Catholic nor the Church of England authorities would consider them an in those days they were the main adoption societies. Their marriage was good and Millie still mourns after twenty years of widowhood.

During the war there was little chance of doing much travelling for pleasure, either home or abroad. As soon as the war was over we went as a family to Brighton for the day. Everybody had the same idea and there were huge queues for the train. It was a beautiful day and the masses of visitors streamed down the High Street to the seafront, which still had barbed wire fence on some of the beaches.

We basked in the sunshine, got very burnt and queued for an hour or so to get onto the train back home. Unfortunately was skin not able to cope with its first dose of sea air and sunshine for six years and I developed herpes around my mouth, causing huge sores. It looked much worse then it was and I was particularly sensitive. I was a prefect at school and had to sit at the head of the table, watching over first formers. Some of them were rather horrible little girls and used to put their unwanted puddings on the floor, under the table when I wasn't looking.

1952 John

After five years of extensive socialising, I decided to develop my career and started to study again. Many of the men were studying to be actuaries, but the course was long and difficult and I choose to study for the Institute Of Chartered Secretaries. The Pru subsidized the course, which included Law, Accountancy and Economics. It was a predominantly male class but I sat with a sociable woman a little older than myself and soon found the subject interesting and enjoyable. Behind us sat two men who joked and one poked me with a ruler. After some weeks we started to talk and he asked me for a date which I accepted.

Sitting behind us were two men who laughed and joked through the Economics class and every so often I got poked with a ruler. Soon we all got quite friendly and around about June one of the men called John asked me out. Up to then I only had a brief friendship with a young man from the Pru, who had just broken up with his fiancée. He was a Catholic, which was an important consideration for me, but was obviously pining for his girlfriend. We struggled out for a couple of weeks and eventually his girlfriend had a change of heart and wanted him back. In some ways I was quite relived, but it was my first romantic experience and gave me a desire for a one to one relationship so John came along at the right time.

By this time, John and I had become quite close to one another and after an inventible split of a couple of weeks we got engaged. As I was a Catholic and John was interested in the religion anyway he started to attend mass in the lunchtimes at the nearest church, which happened to be the old pre-reformation church St. Ethelreda's in Ely Place. Mass was held in the crypt as the main church had blast damage. He then took instructions in the faith from the local parish priest in Hammersmith.

John was ten years older then me, about 5ft 9ins, 11 and a half stone, dark hair with glasses, teeth with a gap between the front two teeth and spoke with a Cockney accent.

His life had not been easy. He, along with his two older brothers were put into care when their split up, leaving his mother with the oldest boy, who was fourteen and able to work. Jon was four years of age and apart from a couple of brief visits, never saw his father again.

CHILDHOOD

Life in the care was vastly different in the 1920's then it is today. The boys were subject to a strict, authoritarian routine. There were no luxuries; food was plain and clothing just adequate. If a boy wet the bed he was made to stand outside, even one cold winter nights. However the matron was a kind, motherly soul and the boys formed a close relationship with her. One of John brother's died whilst sleepwalking but his other brother did well and won a scholarship to the local grammar school. John was equally bright, but four years younger and when his time came he was not allowed to take up a place at grammar school.

In 1917 there were no social services but the orphan and destitute children were cared for by the state. In this particular case the state had taken over one complete side of a road of terraced houses, three up, three down type with outside toilet – twelve houses in all. They had been semi gutted and each two terraced houses joined together, forming as settlement of six homes, each compromising of four upstairs bedrooms – two small, two large – downstairs consisted of one large dining room, one bathroom, one kitchen, one study, one bed sit room and two outside toilets and a large garden. The study and bed-sit was allocated to the House Matron, who also had exclusive use of one of the outside toilets, which was kept scrupulously clean by the boys. The head boy and his deputy had a small bedroom each. The head boy's room was open plan to a large bedroom, where he could easily see and check on the seven youngest children, the deputy similarly connected to another bedroom with the six remaining children.

All the beds were solid iron and steel sprung, solid hard, flock mattresses, the beds of each of the youngest seven had a thick rubber sheet, between the mattress and bottom sheet as a protection from bed wetting, which was a nightly occurrence, with many of the boys, although they were regularly woken by the head boy, to use the potties kept under their beds. A bed wetter was punished by having the wet sheet draped over his head and left in his wet nightie for five or ten minutes, which in mid winter, with no central heating was devastating, yet few boys caught cold.

All the floors of the bedroom were made of plain wood that over the years had became dark brown and highly polished, a result of the boy's chores over the period. Downstairs was a highly polished, thick, dark brown, cork lino, with a carpet centrepiece in the Matrons two rooms. The dining room had a long, heavy wooden table, scrubbed white through the years. At each end sat the head boy and his deputy, with the seven youngest on one side and the remaining six on the opposite side, sitting on long, backless chairs scrubbed white. This constant cleaning meant there was no need for a tablecloth. The matron never ate with the boys.

The bathroom had a large, cast iron bath along one side and on the other side, a kiln like cast, iron boiler, all bricked in with a large, thick wooden lid with a wooden handle. The hot was transported from the boiler to the bath in wooden buckets, filled by a huge wooden handled ladle. The head boy and his deputy did this work every Friday – bath night – under the strict supervision of the house Matron. She bathed the seven youngest herself, by standing them in the large bath and washing each one down. Then they were lifted out by the head boy, who dried them, put on their nighties and dressing gowns, and then sat them on a bench, which ran along the length of the bathroom. This was all completed in thirty minutes, and then the other boys bathed themselves two at a time, sitting at each end of the bath. They were allowed five minutes for each pair, usually finishing about six thirty. Finally the two oldest boys had the luxury of bathing on their own.

Before going to bed at six forty five pm, the youngest had to polish the cutlery for about ten minutes just to get them used to performing the odd jobs. The others dusted and prepared the vegetables for the next few days' meals, then read or played board games until they went to bed at eight o'clock. This left the two head boys, who cleared up then sat in the study with the Matron who gave them their duties for the following day and went to bed about nine pm in the winter and ten pm in the summer, with a hot cup of cocoa and a thick slice of bread and dripping.

Saturday morning all the scrubbing and polishing was done and the two head boys were taught to cook. A boy was made deputy at ten or eleven and a head boy at eleven or twelve, so that by thirteen they were cooking all the Sunday dinners, which gave the Matron a well-deserved rest. She went to early morning services and all fifteen boys went to Sunday school in the afternoon. All the boys were confirmed into the Church of England. They had to join the cub and then the scouts. The annual camp holiday was a great treat for them and presented no problems as they were taught to darn their socks, sew on buttons and wash and iron. Girls at another home laundered the large items, such as sheet and blankets and curtains. Like the boys they learnt a trade at fourteen to sixteen. There were few open jobs to them, mainly domestic help and laundry work. The boys had the choice of tailoring, carpentry, shoe repair and farming areas.

Every child was taught a trade and John learnt shoe repairing and shoe making. Most of the girls in care went into service, which was badly paid but gave them a home.

The farming boys were fortunate as most were sent to Canada where there was a labour shortage; some luckier still were officially adopted by their new employers. John wanted to be a farmer, but the boys were interviewed at fourteen by the Assistant Superintendent at Head Office and only half a dozen of the biggest and strongest boys were chosen and he was not big for his age. The others were allocated to a workshop of one of the trades, in John's case the shoe repairing shop.

At Head Office, sporting activities loomed large and all the boys fourteen years and over had to be involved in one sport or another. Some all-rounders participated in all: cricket, football, boxing, swimming, athletics, and gymnastics and competed the London Federation of Boys Club events. Head Office had a superb hall and gymnasium, together with a first class cricket and football pitch with a professional trainer who was very strict but a fair man. In winter when the football team played away, usually in Hackney marshes he treated all the team to hot dogs and a cup of Bovril.

Sport training was only available in the evenings; mainly on Monday, Wednesday and Thursday as the boys were busy learning their trade during a five-day week. Friday evenings were reserved for light workouts and every Saturday there was some kind of match taking place. Summer training outdoors was very enjoyable but the winter was tough. The footballer had to be proficient with both feet as well as their heads. To achieve this, boys who were naturally right footed were given a pair of thick socks and a left football boot and vice versa for left footed players. Then they had to play a full match on a cold, hard pitch at least once, sometimes twice a week, through the winter. They soon learnt to kick with only with the booted foot as the footballs were leather and the effect on a foot only clad in a sock could be devastating and never attempted more then once. Within no time, all became proficient with their wrong foot so that our team had this great advantage over others. Over the years the Homes Trophy Room became an Aladdin's Cave of Silverware.

At sixteen he was found a job and digs, and with a few meagre possessions set out into the world. His first home was a disaster, as he lodged with a vicar with homosexual tendencies and John gathered his things around him and left. He was truly on his own.

At eighteen he sought out and found his mother, who was living in Shepherds Bush, having acquired another son, some ten years younger then John, but strangely given the same Christian name. He lived with his mother for a short time, until she went to live with a bandleader as his housekeeper in the country. Then he was fortunate to lodge with a motherly welsh woman with two daughters at home and married sons. He fell in love with the oldest girl and they became engaged.

YOUNG MAN

John entered the Home Shoe Shop at fourteen to begin his tuition in the art of making and repairing shoes. It was a single storey; solid brick built building with small windows high up in the walls and solid, double doors, with a steel bar and heavy lock. Set in one of the doors was a smaller door, which was used for entry and departure from the workshop. The double doors were used only for deliveries and dispatches. In winter the small door kept the shop cosy, but in the summer it was stifling. He was fortunate to start with three other boys – kindred spirits, leaving their childhood behind and embracing adulthood.

They were stuck immediately on entering the workshop by an overpowering, pungent smell, which was a combination of glues, chemicals, resins and leather peculiar to all shoe workplaces. There were two rows of solid wooden benches upon which sat at regular intervals sprouted a foot long thick metal spike, behind each with thick, leather aprons, stood boys of various statures and appearance. All had stopped what ever they had been doing to gaze upon the four newcomers to their world. As they looked at these statue like figures a strange sight caught their eye, hopping about on a wooden leg was a man of grimy appearance: wispy, semi bald hair and from his mouth drooped a half chewed, damped, unlit, handmade cigarette, above which was a sparse, ginger moustache. But his whole face excluded warmth, friendliness and utter dependability, with a slight smile, which appeared to be permanent. Later on they were to realise that he was the mainstay for the boys in the shop - the workshop father, confessor, and all things to all men.

The headman was seldom in the workshop. Possibly once a week, for a fleeting visit and to receive a report from Dom, the nickname of the peg legged man. It was also his practise to receive the newcomers and they were taken into his office to listen to a ten-minute discourse on the rules and then hand them over to Dom. They were allocated a number that corresponded to a metal wardrobe, for want of a better word, a tall row of joined boxes, six feet high, with keys. One for the boy and the other for Dom. Inside the lockers were hooks for clothes, dungarees and leather aprons.

The boys took their places at their allocated number on the benches and were introduced to the boy on their right who was to be their overseer for the first three months, sometimes according to a gossip, a fate worse then death. However the group was a reasonable crowd and Dom made certain that there was no bullying in the shop.

The top of each metal spike had a moulded top on which was placed a metal last, shaped like a shoe. The shoe to be repaired was placed on the last and a thick leather strap was attached to the heels and to the boy's own right foot, leaving their hands free to use the tools. There were a many and varied gadgets used that had been handed down from generations of shoe workers. The hours were long compared to their schooldays but John was fortunate in most Tuesdays, in winter he played football. When their trade had been learnt, the boys were prepared for the outside world. They were taken to various shops and workshops in the area where boys from the home had started their careers and moved on to better positions.

John was fortunate to be placed in a husband and wife owned shoe shop, with a large turnover, selling mainly ladies shoes. They had no children and had built up a busy repair trade, which was more then the husband could manage. John was their first boy from the home and for the first year everything went well and he was treated like a son. When the boys had left the home at sixteen, they were given a full set of tools, leather apron, two suits, one for everyday use and the other for best, a pair of boots, pair of shoe, two sets of underwear, toilet accessories, razor, toothbrush, brush and combs etc. They were thus kitted out for their first year.

Along with three or four friend from the home, John bought a bicycle and the boys used to cycle to Southend on a Saturday night, returning on the Sunday night to be ready for work on Monday. In the winter they played football, taking part in the local trade leagues. Most youngster played football in those days and there were abundant pitches and league matches on a Thursday afternoon and Saturdays, for all grade of skill up to professional status. One of their friends had a trial for West Ham, hut was considered to small at five foot, seven. Girls started to play a part in their lives on a Saturday night, along with the cinema, but John's closet friend was a half cast of Chinese extraction and was somewhat cold-shouldered. Consequently they ended up playing billiards or snooker in sleazy halls with cloth worn tables. Chink, as he was called, was restless and wanted to explore the world to see if it had anything better to offer him and he urged John to accompany him.

The couple that employed John gradually improved his responsibilities and his wages from 22/6d to 35 shillings and treated him like a son. He had lunch and tea with them, although not at the same time as shops did not close for lunch in those days and someone had to be left in the shop, and occasionally John was left in the shop, on his own.

He had recently exchanged his old bike for a new, three speed racer, which cost a bomb and the weekly payment were becoming difficult, with the dangers of repossession. There was on one he could turn to and unfortunately began to dip in the till when he was left on his own in the shop. At first only 2/6d then 5/ - and 10/ -. This might have increased but the owner came into the shop one day and caught him taking money from the till. The owner was a good man and sat John down and asked for an explanation, which he gave.

The man with great consternation on his face asked why John had not come to him, particularly as he regarded him as a son. John was so ashamed he could not speak and after work was over he met Chink and both decided to seek their fortunes far away. At ten o'clock that night they cycled away into the night with practically no money and few possessions tied to the back of reaching their bikes, with the intention of reaching Lowestoft where they had spent many happy camping holidays from the home. Not having a map they headed for Chelmsford that they knew and from which Harwich or Ipswich would be signposted. They cycled miles and by the time they reached to him, particularly as he regarded him as a son They cycled miles and by the time they reached Chelmsford were exhausted. With relief they found an old barn and settled on some hay for the night. In the morning, the gruff voice of a farmhand woke them. He advised them to go quickly as the farmer was not of an easy temper. They shot off, managing to take a few carrots from an unsealed sack. The next few nights were spent in the same way, with swedes or potatoes as a change of diet. Eventually they reached Lowestoft and on the second day tried to get casual work on a fishing boat, not realising that all the boats were owned, or skippered by families who had been fishing for generations and only and only employed their own people.

Eventually, after about a fortnight, with no hope of employment and starving hungry, they went to the local Bobby in Kessingland, a small village, outside of Lowestoft. He heard their story, took them to his own, gave them a meal and phoned to the homes. The next day the lodge keeper from the Homes arrived and took the boys back to London. Chink and John were thoroughly dispirited with their adventures.

They were placed in a hostel after a week the Superintendent sent for them and told them new jobs had been found, with lodgings and, as they would soon be eighteen, the Homes would no longer be responsible for them. They were now on their own and no further help would be given. John was sent to a Wood Green lodging and worked in a nearby, small shoe factory. The home never employed their own people. At sixteen he was found a job and digs, and with a few meagre possessions set out into the world. His first home was a disaster, as he lodged with a vicar with homosexual tendencies and John gathered his things around him and left. He was truly on his own.

At eighteen he sought out and found his mother, who was living in Shepherds Bush, having acquired another son, some ten years younger then John, but strangely given the same Christian name. He lived with his mother for a short time, until she went to live with a bandleader as his housekeeper in the country. Then he was fortunate to lodge with a motherly welsh woman with two daughters at home and married sons. He fell in love with the oldest girl and they became engaged.

The next four years John progressed at work, gaining promotion and steady increments and a good job with a fashionable shoemaker in Tottenham Court Road. As digs in that area were very expensive, he found cheap and friendly accommodation with a Welsh family in Shepherds Bush area. There were two girls in the family and John had an instant rapport with the older, which led to their engagement.

Army

It was 1939 and war clouds were gathering and within a few months John was conscripted in the army with the Royal Artillery at Woolwich depot from which he was posted to Larkhill Gunnery Range. Like many other young couples at the time, John and Edith decided to marry before he was posted. After six weeks training he was sent to the Artillery Company stationed at Maidstone M, then on to two months coastal defence practise around Dover and Deal.

It was now 1939 and war had broken out. John knew he would be conscripted and he and Edith married. He joined the Royal Artillery in a tank regiment and had the unfortunate experience to lose a finger, when in trying to stop a runway tank his finger got caught by his signet ring.

He was then moved to Seven Oaks for recalibrating guns ready for overseas combat. The guns were old 1914–18 sixty pounders, which were so heavy and cumbersome that they required a crew of ten to handle them. This post cost John a finger. They were due at Larkhill firing range for recalibrating of their guns, but first the weapons had to have slight modifications, to accommodate more modern sighting equipment and use of the up to date towing vehicle. This was one done locally, one gun at a time. With a team of six including the driver, John arrived at the local workshop and drove into the bay area prior to unhooking the guns. John noticed that they were on a slight slope and asked the Sergeant in charge if they could reposition the gun so it was side on to the slope, thus avoiding any chance of guns running back and forward once it was unhooked from the vehicle. It was a definite possibility as their compliment was six instead of the usual ten. However the Sergeant thought otherwise and as they unhooked, the gun ran backwards.

John was at the eye and his left hand was squashed against the vehicle. Fortunately his instant reaction was to move his hand and his middle finger got squashed into a fleshy pulp. Eight hours later he awoke from an operation minus one finger. He remained in hospital for a week during which time his regiment had gone to Larkhill and he had become unattached. In the next bed was a fellow from Bradford who had been in hospital twelve weeks, recovering from an accident with a tank, which left him one leg, half an inch sorter than the other. He was also unattached and considered that he had the right to visit his parents in Bradford. He invited John to join him and together they discharged themselves one late

Saturday night, knowing on Sunday there would be nobody around to do anything about their disappearance. They had a glorious time in Bradford before the Military Police caught up with them and they were returned to their original units. John never saw his friend again and was punished by unit commander with one month's jonkers, which entailed slopping out latrines, dumping coal and coke to the cookhouse, to the officers and sergeant's mess's, peeling potatoes

In 1940 he was sent to Egypt and joined the Eight Army. They were crammed in the boat going over and some of the men died from the heat exposure. In the desert they were under the control of Field Marshall Montgomery, a great solider whom all his men respected. They fought closely with a Ghurkha regiment and got to enjoy their powerful curriers.

A tragic happening in his life was the death of his wife from pneumonia in the early days of the war. Called back from service, he was numbed and accepted the overseas posting with relief. He spent the rest of the war in North Africa, returning as part of the army occupation in Italy Scilly and Austria.

The primitive conditions in the desert had affected the nerves of his stomach and on his release; he was not able to pursue his trade. Ex servicemen were offered training courses and he took up bookkeeping and typing, which led to an office job. He soon graduated from a clerk to accounts clerk, then on to office manager, and had started studying accountancy when we met.

John and I went out a couple of times and then I took him for tea one Sunday afternoon to meet the family. As I was twenty-four and had never taken a boyfriend home, my family was understandably disturbed at the prospect of meeting John. Dad took an instant dislike to him, my brother wasn't too keen and my mother just about accepted him.

Nothing daunted, we continued going out together, often taking the familiar walk along the riverbanks. Mum was always anxious when I was out at night and by the light of the streetlight I used to see the curtain move in her bedroom window, although it was never later then eleven o'clock. One night I came in crying, the combination of walking with unfamiliar high heels had aggravated a verruca on the ball of my foot. When she saw me, my mum was upset and it took time to persuade her that it was my foot and not John that had caused my tears. There was no need for her anxiety, as I was thoroughly indoctrinated on the sins of sex before married, and had an overwhelming fear of an unwanted pregnancy.

With all the unaccustomed walking, the verruca became more inflamed and painful. It was one of the hazards of swimming that I picked up these contagious warts from the baths. It was the worst one ever, and my chiropodist sent me to the nearest hospital, which was Bart's. After several months of various types of treatment, which often lead me back to the office in pain and tears, there was no improvement and on a return visit to the chiropodist she recommended that I went into the Royal Orthopaedic Hospital, to have it surgically removed.

She worked closely with the late George VI's doctor and he performed the operation. The verruca had spread so badly that it had turned malignant and attached itself to the bone on the ball of the foot. I had stitches and was off work for a couple of moths. To recuperate I went with my mother to Brighton, staying at a Prudential assisted hotel and John joined us for a week. Unfortunately I got the foot wet whilst bathing, which made the removal of the stitches agonizingly painful.

1952 Marriage

In the meanwhile, I applied for one of the Prudential owned flats and to our amazement as housing was hard to obtain, I was offered a flat in Ladbrokes Grove fairly near to where I was born, and very near to Albert and his wife Margaret. These precipitant wedding plans and we arranged to be married on December 20th 1952 at Holy Trinity Church Book Green, where John was receiving instructions. .

It was a small wedding and the registrar was half an hour late, but although it was a damp day it was not excessively cold for December. Most of the photographs were taken at the reception, held at the Milestones Hotel opposite Kensington Gardens. After the reception we went back to the flat followed by some members of the family. For some weird reason and I can't remember why, John decided to finish laying the lino in the kitchen. Never a practical or energetic man where household jobs were concerned, he probably thought it was the best time while the guests were drinking to finish a long overdue task. Needless to say the guests soon disappeared.

The flat was large and Victorian, with a communication system running from the kitchen, where in the past the servants could be summoned. The ceilings were high, the rooms draughty and difficult to keep clean, especially for me, as my mother did every thing at home. She always found it quicker and easier to do it herself. Not being domesticated herself, she never bothered to show me how to cook or look after a house. When I got engaged I started to take cookery classes and did manage to make an additional wedding cake, which supplied my many friends at work, and also savoury dishes, which John ate when he met me from school.

The rent of the flat was quite high and we were fortunate to get another young married couple to share with us. Audrey was a colleague of mine and was married to a Pole, who had served in the Polish air forces based in England. Bron was unused to helping his wife with household chores and was amazed that John cooked, washed up and helped with the housework, but of course John had cooked for himself for many years and was a much better cook then I. The four of us got on very well, but after a year they had a baby daughter and decided to get their own building with a garden.

Marriage did not particular suit me. I did not like cooking, housework or household duties especially as I continued to work and found all the extra chores exhausting. Then again I missed the lively discussions and arguments that we had at home. We were all voluble and excitable, whereas John was inclined to be reticent at home and only lively with company. However we were in love and both of us made efforts to adjust o our new life, although it was soon obvious there was a basic incompatibility. We rowed particularly continuously in our first year of married life and as a young woman I had a tendency to throw things in anger and on one occasion, depositing a plateful of roes over John's suit. My mother aid said I would have been better top have lived in a sin and concentrated on a career, but she waited to tell me this after I was married.

The flat was on the first floor with a steep flight of stairs and a large cellar in the basement. When the murderer Christie was on the run, I used to imagine that he was hiding in the cellar. It was not such an impossible idea, as Rillington Close was only a few minutes walk from us and he was eventually found on the Chiswick towpath where we used to walk when we were courting.

Opposite the flat was the Covent of the Poor Clares and we overlooked their garden where we could see the brown figures tending their vegetable. Like my father before me I got very friendly with one of the nuns of the convent. She was one of the few sisters who had any contact with the outside world, and used to go begging for food in the Portobello road market. The stallholders were good to the nuns and supplied them with their excess food especially vegetable on a Saturday night. The order was enclosed, the nuns leading an austere life of poverty, fasting and prayer, mainly in silence. They had no heating or electricity, as the reverend mother at the time was frightened of it. They were highly thought of in the district and received many letters from people all over the country requesting their prayers.

Sister Teresa was a friendly chatty soul who was the only survivor of a family of 13 children, all who died in infancy. The convent had a beautiful little chapel with a large statue of St Francis of Assisi and the nuns received communion from a grill behind the altar.

We attended Mass there on Sundays and I often attended during the week. From a window in the flat we could see the nuns in the garden and sometimes saw a nun in a beautiful wedding dress in preparation for her final profession into the Poor Clares. They moved some time later to a convent in Barnet, which I visited some years later, but I always kept in touch with Sister Teresa.

1954 Children's Birth

By the time Audrey and Bron had left with their baby I was also pregnant. Still continuing to work, I travelled up to Farrington Street from Ladbrokes Grove until a few months before Paul was born, fortunately not showing my pregnancy until the latter stages.

I was booked into the Westminster Hospital, which proved difficult for parental visits but excels for the actual birth, which came after 48 hours in labour. The small medical room was full of people, doctors, medical students, a midwife and nurses, but I missed the delivery as I was given chloroform. Although apparently a normal delivery I found the whole experience terrifying and if I had not been a Catholic there would have been no more babies.

The hospital was in the centre of Westminster and catered for the M.P.s and their wives

It was also attended by clergy from the Cathedral. In those days people were expected to fast from midnight before receiving

Communion. The priest who came to me was annoyed that I had eaten at 5-30 a.m. but the sister in charge pointed out that I had to feed my baby. After some heated words between them, he gave me Communion

As we would be restricted for entertainment when the baby arrived, we decided to buy a television set - black and white of course. In 1954 television was a luxury, rather than a necessity for a home. In my temporary absence in hospital John found the set highly entertaining and when we arrived home with Paul a healthy 8lb.2 oz baby, I found the cot and baby bath had not been assembled. However with my mothers helped, we bathed Paul and put him to bed only to find he cried incessantly. Someone in the office had given me a dummy for a joke and in desperation I put it in his mouth and eventually we got some rest. This behaviour pattern continued until he was nearly two.

I had a huge coach type pram with large wheels. It looked impressive but it was awkward to get up and down the stairs. There were no washing machines on the market and I boiled the nappies in a gas boiler. They came up beautifully white, but detergents powders were just on the market and my first use of Tide gave Paul a terrible nappy rash, probably due to inadequate rinsing and ringing out, using a mangy manually operated. Washing day was quite a mammoth task and the wet washing was hung on a pulley-operated clotheshorse suspended from the kitchen ceiling. However I was soon steeled into a routine and took Paul along to the local baby clinic weekly, where I met and made friends with other young mothers.

Paul did not put on weight easily. He was an active energetic boy who had little interest in food. In all he wasn't an easy baby at all and it was with some trepidation that I found when he was seven months old that I was pregnant again.

As with Paul I had quite a good pregnancy, but this time I was fortunate to have an easy delivery and my daughter Hilary was born three weeks late on April 4TH after a few hours in labour. The tax position was such at the time that John got back most of the tax he had paid in the year. Life with two young babies was hard. It was difficult to air the clothes and get them up and down the stairs and into the pram.

When seven moths after Hilary's birth I found myself pregnant again, we decided to buy a house with a garden. Somehow we scraped together the deposit money and we moved to a small house in Kenton Harrow. It was a disastrous move. I missed my parents, my friends, Notting Hill and Portobello Road. It had been too early for me to make friends in the area. Anyway it was a very suburban and middle class, with most people being wrapped up in their own lives. Even the church was distant and unfriendly; so different form St Francis and the little convent.

Shortly after we moved in I fell down the stairs carrying Hilary in my arms. I hit the nursery gates at the bottom and blacked out. It was sometime before I was able to phone John to come home. The children were all right and no harm came to the baby I was expecting, but my nervous system suffered badly. Some months later Nicholas was born in September in Hammersmith Hospital, as was Hilary.

My waters broke during the nigh and I had to travel in the ambulance by myself and John had to look after the other babies.

He was born on the trolley going into the labour room and shrieks of laughter from the nurses as he was a face presentation and they were amused to see a little mouth instead of a head. The other women in the ward were not exactly conventional, their language was appalling, and they smoked incessantly and had terrible rows with the sisters. They treated me as a confidant and intermediary with the sisters. I was physically fitter and used to take their babies back to the nurses while they rested.

1957 Breakdown

However with three young children under four, away from my family and friends and no help my health deteriorated rapidly a few weeks after the birth with severe post natal depression. I struggled on, taking heavy doses of various drugs, but it become a nightmare for me to go out and I used to tremble with fear outside the shops. During the day I often experienced panic attacks and often phoned John to come home, as I couldn't cope.

Within six months I was admitted to a mental hospital. There was several young mothers in the ward and we were told that childbirth cases were the most difficult to cure. Sure enough some patients went home, only to return within days. One unfortunate had even tried to commit suicide. She had tried for years to have a baby and then when it arrived she could not cope. After treatment she returned home only to return to hospital in a worse state. I believe the treatment for post natal depression has improved greatly today and relies more on hormonal remedies rather than tranquilisers.

It was not an entirely unhappy situation as patients we got on very well with each other and could sympathise and console one another. One young girl of 17 could not sleep and no drug could help her. An older woman, probably suffering from the DT's, used to regularly say she could see a large black bear. We used to take walks through the grounds which were rather depressing.

I did not have the comfort of my religion, as I was too anxious to attend the Roman Catholic chapel. Another young RC mother had similar problems. John could not visit me as he had the children to look after, but my father came as often as he could. Even in rail strikes when it took him hours to get to the hospital. After two doctors and various drugs, I was physically fit and felt well enough to discharge myself and return home. After a few weeks I was back where I started a found I could not manage, so I went to my parents rather than return to the hospital, which could not guarantee an improvement in my health. Basically I had lost confidence in my compatibilities as a mother due to physical fatigue and a deep-rooted fear of pregnancy. A very devout Catholic I reject any suggestion that I practised birth control and John as a convert, strictly adhered to the teachings of the church.

My mother was distressed by my illness and found it difficult to accept that I had left three young children, one a young baby. At first I found it hard to go out and could only manage a few hundred yards at time, gradually improving as time went by. Enclosed spaces terrified me; I even had to leave the toilet door open. I was a walking mess of fears and after a while my mother persuaded to get a job near home to take my mind off my anxieties, which fortunately worked. My health gradually improved but I suffered a severe setback when I realised as a result of my stay in Kenton that I was pregnant again. This time I thought I would never get better and would spend the rest of my life in a mental hospital. I didn't tell my parents for sometime and I never told my work colleagues as I could not face being left on my own at home as my mother worked. They were nine months of hell, as I could see no future for myself.

John was unsympathetic and when I could manage to travel to Kenton he was morose, not even bothering to make me a cup of tea, although I was heavily pregnant by that time. He had of course severe problem of his own looking after the children and coping with his work. He lost one job due to commitments with the children. Nicky was at a nursery and the other two at a day nursery. Although a devout Catholic, I have always been amazed at the lack of any support of help from the church, particularly at times when it has been most needed. The situation is improving now; with the greater participation of the laity and various lay organisations. Then again there were no back up facilities for the doctors, no social workers, only a few health visitors and I never got one at Kenton.

My weight increased rapidly but all over my body and no one guessed that I was pregnant. A week or so before the baby was due my leg swelled to twice its size and I was admitted to Hammersmith Hospital again. It was phlebitis, the leg was very painful and I was not allowed out of bed for a fortnight after which the birth was induced. Although Christopher was ten pounds he was not a difficult delivery but I had physiological problems. John obviously could not cope with another baby and I was still lacking in confidence. My mother said she would gave up work to look after the baby so I took him home and returned to work waiting for the inevitable breakdown but it never came. Christopher gave me back my confidence to be a mother but it became increasingly hard to visit Kenton with a new baby. Then again I had another setback when my mother became and ill and cancer of the womb was diagnosed.

My experiences of Hammersmith Hospital were never good, apart from Hilary's birth and the hospital. When Nicky was born all the maternity wards were overcrowded, there were women in beds in the corridors, there were no baby clothes and we laid in blood stained sheets, as there was a shortage of linen.

With Christopher I received no counselling, although they knew my medical history, until after the birth. Then I was referred to a psychiatrist after a few months of regular sessions the he told advised me that to return to my husband and other children would be a mistake, but also not to do would be unsatisfactory but left the decision up to me and discharged me.

In the meanwhile Mum was haemorrhaging but would not go to a doctor. Eventually she became weak the Dad sent for a doctor. She was admitted to hospital and sent home after test. One night the phone rang; it was the hospital advising her to go in for an operation. Mum refused and the doctor told her bluntly on the phone that she had cancer and would live with a surgical treatment, but they did not tell her that even with an operation her life expectancy was short. She was devastated and sat by the phone crying. It was an awful way to treat a human being.

It was a six-hour operation and they removed the womb and also the bladder. The wound in her stomach never healed and her quality of life was poor. It was a cruel operation and she was desperately unhappy. Dad and I managed as best we could to nurse her. I continued to work but came in at lunchtime. Fortunately I had an excellent baby-minder for Christopher and he was a very good baby and rarely cried. John brought the children over to visit, but it was not a good atmosphere for them.

Within a year she was re-admitted to Hammersmith Hospital with secondary cancer that had gone into the bloodstream. By this time Christopher was nearly two and together we were regular visitors to the hospital, but it was a cancer ward and I used to shake with fear as I waited to go in. the patients loved to see Christopher and made a fuss of him. Mum was a marvellous patient and never complained, often refusing morphine. Her weight dropped to around four stone before she died, but she had fought the disease for as long as she could. I had lost quite a bit of weight myself and was at low ebb. It was not surprising therefore that I felt unable to go the cemetery, but I attended the requiem mass in the small church. A large new church was in process of being built and work continued during the mass.

I stayed to look after Dad, but as my health gradually improved I knew I would have to take over the family again, so we started to look for houses in the Shepherds Bush area. Forsaking my churches teachings on birth control I had the coil fitted and as John would not give his permission I forged his signature for the first and only time in my life. At first we looked for a suitable house for us all, but my father and husband did not get on too well, so Dad stayed put and we found a nice house in East Acton.

The fear of childbirth being removed, I was able to concentrate on bringing up the family, although I still continued to work.

The small printing firm I worked for were helpful when the children were ill and I was allowed to take work home. It was a friendly, happy firm and I made several friends, but they ran in financial difficulties and were taken over by an American company. The atmosphere changed and Dad advised me to apply for at job at Wormwood Scrubs Prison, where he worked as a carpenter.

1966 Prison

There was a clerical post vacancy and after an interview I was accepted by the Home Office, subject to an extensive medical examination. My illness caused much agony and suffering but was often lightly dismissed by many people I came into contact with, possibly because I worked extremely well.

As my mental health improved I started driving lessons after buying a large, second hand car from a man at work. It was a Humber and very comfortable with leather seats but the garage was on a bend at the end of the drive and was practically impossible to get it in the garage, especially by an inexperienced driver. The gears were in the wheel and my driving instructor finally persuaded us to get another car. John had driven a tank during the war but had no experience of cars and after we brought a little Austin A 35 van, started to take lessons as well. The boys by now were old enough to really enjoy our new activity. I passed my driving test on the second attempt just before I moved to the prison.

Dad had worked for the prison for a few years as a carpenter assisted by a team of prisoners. Having being brought up in Notting Hill, he was well used to the criminal element and had his own code of ethnics. If his employers were wealthy or a big concern he would come home with tins of paint, nails, timber, much to my mothers horror, but he used to say they left over from the job. This of course not possible in the prison service but it was quite surprising the number of things that did disappear. It was said that the large grand piano brought in for Ivor Novello when he was a prisoner disappeared having been taken out of the gates for tuning.

It was 3rd of January 1966, my first day at the prison. I was escorted through the gates and taken to the office block just inside in a large courtyard. It was a modern block and the offices were warm (most of the time) and comfortable. There was a good community spirit in the prison, although some rivalries between the three main sections - the officer governor class, the Works department and the Civilian staff and clerical staff. It always appeared that the central heating was serviced and repaired in winter.

I was allocated to the manufacturing department and was placed in a large, airy room with another officer, instructor's wife and elderly man and an executive officer, who had just transferred from a small, seaside prison and was a little discontent and used to extol the merits of his former prison. The elderly man lived in the bachelor quarters within the prison. It was cheap but had it snags in that he was supposed to be in by eleven o'clock pm and he moaned about the tea, as he was convinced that it contained bromide. John who worked for a tea and coffee firm agreed that the contract for the services did contain a drug.

In the office we brought our own cups of tea in and the cons used to make it for us; usually managing to break at least one cup a week. In desperation I took in a virtually unbreakable cup, but it soon went the way of the others. For meals we could either use the mess in the prison, or the officers club outside, which had a bar and provided light refreshments, but I used to cycle home.

My job was to order materials for some of the prisons workshops and to arrange for the dispatch of the goods made, and the invoicing. There were several shops but I used to work mainly in the bookbinders. These were the days before Blake escaped and I used to wander over the shops during the course of the day to check with the instructors. In first three months I was asked to undertake a stock take on two stocks, one of them the bookbinders. Never very technical it was a daunting task for me as there was a range of knives and tool and various materials. It was quite an important task, although obviously the knives were checked at the end of each working day.

The shops were cleared of the inmates, but the bookbinder had a trusty with him. Working with them I managed to check the inventory, but it took some hours. I settled in quickly into the community; my father was very popular and the civilian men extend this friendship to me, even to the extent of treating me as one of them. I was amused one day to be asked by the plumber to look after one of his men for a few minutes, which was repairing the incinerator in the ladies toilet. He seemed a pleasant young man and we chatted while he worked. When I asked the plumber what he was in here for I was shocked when he replied "for rape." Possibly he was only joking but I didn't pursue it. Latter I found the crime rarely fitted the inmate, and the devoted father whose daughter visited him regularly could be in for incest and the murderers were pleasant, good-tempered men.

The relax atmosphere was soon dispelled by the escape of George Blake the counter spy. Dad knew him quite well as did many of the staff, as he wandered round the prison, a trusted inmate, a nod found him a friendly, charming man. Everybody was under suspicion after the escape and life inside was never the same. The Mountbatten report recommended sweeping changes which were soon implanted: inner gates were installed and we could no longer walk through the prison, barbed wire and security cameras went up on the perimeter walls and guards dogs were brought in. The inmates were more restricted and lost a lot of their freedom.

I moved after a while into the wages office. It was a hard-pressed office as most officers then were paid in cash and their money had to be ready by Thursday. They did considerable overtime, all at different rates, but they were appreciative when we rushed through pay rises and bank holiday money and used to give us chocolate once I was given an iced birthday cake. In those days each man had national insurance card that had a weekly stamp on it. These rates changed and sometimes this was not discovered until the stamp was on the card. It was strictly illegal to remove these stamps, but our boss used to send us up to the small kitchens to get one of the inmates to steam them off usually with the warning not to go inside with the men. It was a nightmare at the end of the financial year, preparing P60's, which was all done manually.

It was difficult moving from the wages office as no one wanted to do it, but after two years one could I ask for move and I successfully applied and was moved to what was known as the Discipline office, which was purely prison work. The staff had to work out the sentence and if there were an error and an inmate kept overtime; he was entitled to compensation, which could be taken from the officer concerned. The inmates could petition the Home Office and the Strasbourg Court of appeal and they did so regularly. It was my to get the papers together, ready for the governor's signature and then dispatch them. The petitions were not censored apart from the language and they together with the files could make pretty harrowing reading. On top of that I acted as a relief clerk to the Board of Visitors. This entailed taking down in longhand all the dialogue between the magistrates, inmates and officers in adjudication hearing. The prisoners were not taken out the prison for misdemeanours unless they were very severe and were punished inside the prison, usually by loss of remission. These sessions took place in a wing in the prison and one such case went on for much longer then usual, ending up with a severe punishment which must have reached the ears of the inmates of the wing before we left and we were greeted with a barrier of hostile silence as we walked back through the dining room in the wing. It was quite frightening and both magistrates were fairly old men and we only had two officers with us. The room was long and seemed to take us ages to get through.

As well as my work in the prison I was looking after a house, husband and four children. There were few problems with the children; Christopher had been brought up by me for a few years and had most of my attention plus a doting grandfather, Nicky had been in John's care plus nurses in a day clinic. They were both a bit spoilt and resented one another and they did not like sharing a parent with another person albeit their own father and mother. Christopher started to stammer and both developed behaviour problems. Unfortunately I did not have the required patience to deal with the situation. An Irishwoman from the church looked after them when they came in from the school and during the school holidays and sickness and we became good friends. We became more involved in the church, which had a very large Irish population, who created a lively, friendly community. The parish priest was a good friend of ours. He was gentle and kind and tolerant. It was an unfortunate time for the church where a more liberal approach was being promulgated. This combined with the new permissive society made any of the priests and nuns restless and there was an exodus of religion to get married.

Hilary had a very strict headmistress, about fifty years of age who was very tough with the girls. With the relaxation on clothes, her skirt became shorter and shorter, he veil sat further back on her head and the eventually the habit disappeared altogether and the nuns wore ordinary clothes and makeup. Even their names were changed and they adopted their original Christian names. It all happened too suddenly and when Hilary came home rather upset there were rumours of the headmistress having an affair with a parish priest of a nearby church, I was not surprised. The rumours were confirmed later and they were married much to the consternation of the girls who found it difficult to accept middle aged man and woman could give everything to marry. They were all young enough to find it all rather disgusting.

Our local church was being rebuilt and a brand new social club was added alongside. It opened up an active social club for John and me. The parish priest had three curates, one of which had been recently ordained and he was energetic and took over the running of the club. It was very successful, there was a large hall, a bar area, a fruit machine and a hall upstairs. There were groups playing each week, many with a string Irish folk dance influence and we joined in energetically with old Irish favourites such as the Siege of Ennis. John was very keen on dancing and insisted on the leading the dance and he also took to the fruit machine with great vigour, often spending hours playing on them. The young priest spent too much time on the club that he found it quite hard to get up in time for mass in the morning. It probably wasn't the best training for a priest and eventually he left to get married. The new social life was a novelty for us and we drank, smoke and gambled too much and left the children to their own devices, although the came with us when we went racing. Where we lived we could reach most of the racecourse fairly easily. John by now was a company secretary and had a firm's car and we made good use of it travelling around the country, usually taking Dad with us.

We were out so much that I did not realise that Christopher was unhappy at school and began truanting. He never did like school and developed an aversion, as he got older. His truanting got so bad, that we gave up a lot of social activities and finally decided to move to Leigh on Sea, where Albert and his wife were living. I had been moved to the Borstal Section at the prison and found the reports on the boys upsetting and disturbing. The final straw came when I left my office one day to see a young boy on the roof, waiting to jump. He had been up there a couple of hours and no one could persuade him to come down. As I walked across the courtyard he looked at me and the first thing I saw in the morning was a crushed flowerbed and I knew that he had jumped.

I had management problems in the prison as I was an active union member and fought for woman rights. There were virtually no promotions for woman in those days. It was predominately a man's world but the women did the same work as the men in the office, but we were definitely second-class citizens. The Civil Service itself however was a good job as we received equal problem with the men, which quite a few outside jobs did not.

I had also started studying again; this time criminology and my course fees and books were mainly paid for by the service. The course was very interesting and mainly attended by prison staff and police, and led to a successful completion and a Certificate in Criminology. John attended the Sociology classes with me and we an excellent tutor in Phillip Bean. It was a three-year course and required a great deal of study but it was relevant to my work.

1972 Old Bailey

I applied for a move and was posted to the Old Bailey. It was a vastly different world from the prison services. The Civil Service had recently taken over the Court system and in doing so had to give officers of the court ranks in accordance with their pay and the pay in the Old Bailey was high, thus there were many high ranking officers and few of the lower ranks. The men work dark grey suits and women working the courts wore black. I was in the Treasurer's office and worked out witnesses and juror's expenses. It was a small office, with three of us calculating the expenses.

The journey to the Old Bailey was straightforward and I took the central line from East Acton to St Paul's. There were grave snags with the job in that we had to wait until the case had finished and some of them went on until very late. or rarely overnight. We were not paid overtime but could claim extra free time. As well as that the cash had to balance every night to a penny. It could take hours to find a ten pence error. There was a good restaurant in the building and a friendly atmosphere. When a case was running late we went into the court to listen to the final stages and the summing up. Life became very difficult when we moved to Leigh. At the time there were a series of strikes on the trains and we often had to get out of the train at an earlier station and then get a bus.

My colleague was a Nigerian new to Britain .He was shocked by British society and the way the women dressed

 women dress   He had his wife and youngest child with him but said he would not bring the older children

 here , in case they in case they were corrupted were corrupted. His father had several wives and as the oldest son he had a duty to son had the duty to always care for his mother. We worked well together although his

               English was poor..

When I was settled I decided to go ahead with my criminology studies and after I passed the Certificate started on a thesis for the Diploma. The subject I chose was the Young Offender. My appointed tutor was a psychiatrist at the Maudsley Hospital.

The travelling was extensive as I already had the journey to work and after work the journey to London. However I completed the thesis but it was not successful. That was not surprising as the statistics were subject to the Official Secrets Act and also it was too emotive a subject for me .

The Old Bailey was a glamorous and exciting world with many of the defendants and witnesses being famous people. My friends were keen to meet me for lunch in the restaurant. It was the best job I ever had and if I had been a single it

would have been a career for me. However due to family
commitments I had to move .

1973 Leigh-on-sea

We were familiar with Leigh as My Aunt Margaret and Uncle Albert, my father's brother moved there in 1956, and we visited frequently .During the summer holiday's I used to take Hilary and Christopher for a short stay while John took Paul and Nick on fishing trips.

Leigh is an old fishing port mentioned in the Doomsday book. It is well known for the cockle and whelk fishermen and their little boats are a familiar sight on the Thames. Albert and Margaret spent most of the summer sitting by and bathing in the water. When we moved down I used to join them whenever it was possible. Margaret will be 100 years old next July. She is fairly well but has Ahlzeimers disease. We used to swim from March to November. It is amazing how one can adapt to the cold. A little crowd of pensioners used to meet daily and we had a little party at the end of the season

In 1973; Paul was nineteen, Hilary seventeen, Nicky sixteen and Christopher fourteen. Paul was never any trouble; he was not academic but was quite good with his hands and plodded on well at school with no behaviour problems. He left school at sixteen and became apprenticed to a car mechanic. He had a steady girlfriend, a Catholic girl with a very strict father who unfortunately did not like Paul, which made their relationship difficult. Hilary was struggling with 'A' levels; much more academic then her brothers, nevertheless she found extensive studying exhausting but she had several close friends who eased the tension. Nicky and Christopher both at problems at school which led to a change of school, but it was mainly Christopher who thoroughly disliked school, who had great problems such as truanting. It worried John and me so much that we felt we had spent too much tome at the social club and not enough on our children and we gave up a lot of our activities. Eventually we moved to Leigh take Christopher away from some of his undesirable friends.

The move was not easy to transport: four children, a dog and a cat. I went on ahead with Hilary and stayed with my aunt. The house was tall and rambling and not in a good condition. It was an executor sale and the garden looked as if it had been touched in years - the weeds were waist high. The three oldest children were the wrong ages to move. All their friends were in London and in a few years they all returned to London. Christopher was fifteen and he started his new school and he made a few friends, but in no time was truanting again and it was a great relief when he was sixteen and could start work. Hilary passed her 'A' levels and secured a place in Essex University but it was easier to travel from London by public transport. Paul started work in local garage and Nicky continued working in London. However there was always trouble with the trains, which often made him late for work. The travelling also made life difficult for me as well..

1973 VAT

In a few months I applied for an executive travel in Customs and Excise in Southend, the headquarters of VAT, and was a successful. We moved to Leigh in September 1974 and I started at the VAT H.Q in January 1975, in the post opening section on the ground floor. It was a vast change from the glamour of the Old Bailey. VAT had started in 1973 and was still chaotic. It was huge paper factory with sacks of returns and cheques declared every day. My section was a band of ten older women who happily sorted out the mail daily. It was boring, routine work but they were well established in dealing with the queries and enjoyed one another company.

I was fairly superfluous as an executive officer and in fact when the staff inspectors came they cut us down by half. From the post opening I was moved several times to various sections, none of which I found particularly interesting and finally arrived in the prosecution office where defaulting trader were dealt with, some by the courts. We worked in small sections under a higher executive officer. Most of the senior grades were staffed by men. Customs and Excise had always been predominately male and when VAT was introduced it provided an instrument for promotion for many men. There was nearly 2000 staff in the VAT building, mostly women. The men were not used to dealing with female staff and liaisons were rife and many marriages were broken. As I passed the Certificate in Criminology in 1974 I went on to undertake another thesis for the Diploma, and applied for permission from the Controller as the title was The Screening of Customs Regulations for Prosecution. My work in the Prosecution Department gave me access to statistics and knowledge of the system. My tutor on this occasion was a lecturer at the London School of Economics. Once again I had to travel up to London to see him but it was not as tiring as before and the subject free from personal attitudes. I was successful in 1977 but Customs objected as the subject matter was confidential and infringed the Official Secrets Act.

The problem they said was that the thesis would be available in the University Library as were other thesis . After some correspondence and an appeal the Controller passed it and I was granted the Diploma. When I saw the thesis some sentences had been deleted

Maybe it was a coincidence but later Vat offences were not treated as criminal offences

.

Soon I took a post on the union committee; that again was male dominated and women had very little say. This lead me to a direct confrontation with the union leaders and I took them to a Sex Discrimination Tribunal, which I lost but not too long after that the leader were all replaced and there was a more up to date attitude. A lot of time in Alexander

House during the three years I spent there was taken up on strike action against the poor pay. For the married woman the money was often a second source of income but for men with a family it was a struggle to keep a head above water. Not being particularly strike-conscious myself I often took supporting action in sympathy with the men, and on odd occasions picket duty. There is one thing one soon learns in the Civil Service, that you can't beat the Establishment.

After a few years I applied for a post as a VAT Inspector and was successful. After completing an extensive training program .As I had an intermediate certificate for Company Law the program was not difficult. On completion of the course I was transferred to Romford. It was only about 3/4 hr. from Leigh, but the traffic could be horrendous, and added to this there could be severe weather problems. Being a VAT Inspector involved a lot of travelling, plus my own journey to work. Fortunately another officer lived in Leigh and used to give me a lift .when our duties allowed. Also I had no problem with my car as John as a director was given a new car every few years plus servicing.

There were strict checks on our work, and it could be irritating to finish a visit and preparing to drive home when a senior officer arrived and went through the books again.

Most of the visits were some miles from Romford usually in the opposite direction from Southend. It was stressful and I had to attend the hospital for a biopsies on my breast which fortunately was benign. But my stitches made driving uncomfortable at times.

VAT inspections were lengthy and time consuming. It involved going through all the accounts up to the trial balance. When it was obvious there was a discrepancy we had to examine bank accounts. Public houses were always difficult and to arrive at final figures could mean calculating how many drinks had been poured from spirit bottles. There could also be problem of free drinks for staff .

It was surprising the number of traders whose accounts were chewed by the dog, lost, burnt, soaked in a flood, torn up by the children etc. Then we had to work from purchases and bank statements. Most traders were helpful and writing up accounts can be difficult especially those with no experience of book keeping. Many did rely on accountants which could be expensive. The visits varied and we were usually given a small area to work in. Then again the incidence of a breakdown in the heating system was not uncommon

In one small working man's café, I was put in a little cubby hole with the owner and given a large box to sit on. As I was working a woman came in and asked for some sugar. The owner asked me to get up as I was sitting on the sugar

Another visit to a small off licence I had to work on a table where the remains of the last meal had been left and what was worse was that her cats were on the table eating the left overs. She gave the appearance of being alcoholic, the place was filthy and I felt sorry for her. She gave me a cup of tea which had grease floating on the top. In the end I said I would get in touch with her accountant

In another inspection I was shown into a luxurious flat with low chairs and tables.

The trader, a good looking blond young man came and offered me a cup of tea.

First he said he was going to have a shower. This surprised me as his appearance was meticulous, and he wore a gleaming white shirt. However I assumed he had been rushing and was sweating

He put his accounts on a low table and went for his shower. It didn't take me long to find out they were seriously in error, and would take hours to examine. He the came out dressed in a very short kimona and sat opposite me and starting chatting, so I asked for the tea. He went to make it and I gathered the books up, made out a receipt, and told him that because of the work involved they would be examined in the office. This was a correct procedure if the inspection involved would take several hours. He was furious and became insulting so I left without the tea.

Subsequently I sent him a hefty assessment. He appealed but fortunately appeals had to be examined by another officer. The assessment was confirmed then he started ringing up but my colleagues told him I was out of the office and that he could speak to a senior officer

he then stopped ringing

The travelling and work made me long for my retirement. My ideal was to live in Spain and sunbathe and swim daily. John and I discussed this at length and he wanted to live in the country where he could spend the time fishing. We then decided to have a trial separation, and I moved into a small flat It was not a good move as it was strange for me to be on my own. John used to visit bringing the dog. One visit he was upset as he had been diagnosed with a cataract and we both realised living together had many compensations.

We then looked for a bungalow near the Church in Leigh. It took sometime to find one suitable, John by then had retired and found life difficult. My retirement was close so I applied to get back to the Local VAT Office. Travelling was much easier and we enjoyed a social life in Church activities.

My senior officer was a considerate man both to his staff and to traders. His wife held a senior position in Customs ,they were Catholics and we were friends.

He like many ex Customs officers was a heavy drinker which the work entailed. Where the trader had a large turnover and, or complex VAT ratings, an executive officer had to be accompanied by a senior officer. On one such visit the accounts were very complicated and we spent several hours examining the books. He then suggested we went to lunch which invariably meant the local pub. I had a small lager and he had a pint. Then he suggested another drink . As I didn't particularly like beer, I asked for a whiskey and offered to pay.

He had a beer and a chaser and we sat outside in the sunshine discussing the case and not really coming to a conclusion.. We had both worked in the division dealing with complex issues and knew it could sometimes take weeks to sort out a difficult case. WE returned to the trader and spent another hour or so working on the accounts, then gave up and referred the case to HQ. These difficult cases were interesting and challenging.

I entered VAT at its inception   and obviously the system has changed considerably now.

This is true of my two other Government departments. I joined The Prison Service in 1966 when they had just been taken over by the Home Office. Similarly in 1972 the Old Bailey had been taken over by the Lord Chancellor's Office. New Departments create new structures and some teething problems. My experiences were relevant to those periods. The escape of George Blake from the Prison subsequently led to drastic changes

The main change in the Civil Service is the tremendous improvement in the treatment of women which had been a major source of contention for me, although I did receive equal pay   .

1987 MEDJUGORJE

It was with trepidation that I set off at 6.25am to catch the minibus outside Our Lady of Lourdes Church. Stories of supernatural happenings, horrendous climbs up steep hills and mountains, and primitive living accommodation filled me with apprehension.

The minibus arrived on time at 6.30am. There were 13 of us and we made good steady progress until we reached the inevitable hold ups near Heathrow. Finally we arrived at the airport at 9.30am which left plenty of time to have a coffee before take off at 11.30. As often happens the plane was delayed an hour and my nervous tension increased. At one stage I toyed with the idea of not going at all. At last boarding was announced. As we walked through a customs official decided I looked nervous and searched my handbag thoroughly commenting that I should take water with the miniature whiskey bottle that I carry for emergencies. By this time we were too late to go into the duty free shop where I had intended to buy my husband some Old Holborn tobacco and a small bottle of whiskey for myself for medicinal purpose. It so happened that I developed a very heavy cold within days, but there were at least 4 duty free shops in Medjugorje and I got my whisky and tobacco. There were several of us with colds and the whisky went down well. The plane a Boeing 727 was spacious and the flight was comfortable. We landed at Split at 3pm. The airport is in a lovely position on the coast and the weather was beautiful. We were directed to a waiting coach to take us to Medjugore There was a short delay as we waited for some of our fellow travellers who had obviously found time to visit the duty free shop.

The coach took a picturesque route along the Adriatic Coastline. After about quarter-an-hour the coach suddenly stopped, the back door swung open and up walked the driver. In the back sat the late arrivals a large family group still very merry. After a heated exchange we gathered that smoking was not allowed on the coach .The journey recommenced, but the family group being typically British were soon smoking again the coach pulled up this time on a narrow coast road holding up the following traffic. One of the group muttered that there must be a sensor device in the front of the coach to detect smoke. The driver marched up to the back and it appeared from the tone of his voice that he was preparing to abandon the coach. Our courier a quietly spoken young man then came to the rescue. He pacified the driver and made the family promise not to smoke any more.

The coach set off once more and the courier then started a long discourse on communism and the joys of collective farming. No one felt inclined to argue finer points after the smoking episode. After several hours we pulled up at a cafe for coffee. They did not appear to be expecting us and it took some time before we were served with tiny cups of sweet black bitter coffee which left a thick sludge in the bottom of the cups. Before leaving we visited the toilets, unisex, and met a situation that was to follow in Medjugorje namely a shortage of cubicles, wet floors and a powerful odour. After a lengthy queue we finally made our way back to the coach. It was now dark and we were another hour or so before we reached Medjugorje.

The coach load was divided into little groups who were put off at various points in the village. A very noticeable thing about Medjugorje at night is the lack of electricity power. There are no street lights and the housed are dimly lit. Our house was newly built for pilgrims. These houses are built at incredible speed to accommodate the increasing number of pilgrims. MY little group was shown upstairs where there were three bedrooms for pilgrims. I was put in a room with two other women in a room with three beds a medium size wardrobe and no tables or chairs. The beds, mattresses, duvets and carpet were all new and proved to be very comfortable. Two nuns shared another room, leaving the third room for a middle aged couple and their 27 year old son, Father and son were both over 6ft and conditions must have been cramped. The mother said the next -time they came she would put her son's age on the booking form. I don't suppose that would make any difference.

Every day at 10am there was an English Mass. This got extremely crowded due to the large American presence In Medjugorje The only way to get a seat was to get in a half an hour early and sit through a Mass in another language, and take a seat when they left. It was often so hot and crowded that I sat on the benches outside listening to the Mass on the loudspeakers. Each day, after the Mass at 11am, we met our courier to learn the schedule for the day.

On our first day we were going to visit the house of Vicka a young woman to whom the Virgin Mary appears every night. It was apparently quite a long walk and it was suggested that the not so able got a taxi. There are fleets of taxis in Medjugorje. Each fare was always £2 and they carried 4 passengers. They went at great speed along the narrow roads and if they could not turn round they drove in reverse until they could. It was rather like being in a dodgem car at the fair. A friend and I and 2 others took a taxi, but unfortunately we missed tile rest of our group and got crushed into Vick's garden with a large American group. They were equipped with cine camera and with all the latest technological equipment in photography. Vicka stood on an outside staircase leading to the top of her house. The garden had a lattice like roof covered in grape vines. An attractive and quite glamorous young woman interpreter then asked for questions. Both she and Vicka smiled a lot and were friendly to the questioners. These sessions must be very tiring for Vicka who is suffering from a brain tumour. The questions varied from the trite to the more profound. Most of what Our Lady has told Vicka has been documented and there were no great surprises in the answers. She spoke of her visions of Heaven and Hell. After about 20 minutes the questioning stopped and she went indoors to rest. As she went in one group struggled out and another pushed in. I got one of the waiting taxis and returned to the church.

Near the church is an official shop allowed by the communists selling religious objects. It is very small and to get in it is difficult. There were several assistants giving change in all currencies. We paid for our purchases and left the shop. People were still looking at the sun and we joined them. It was quite difficult to describe, but it appeared to be covered by a large white disc which took away all the brilliance and it was possible to stare at it. I saw black beads surrounding the sun. This was also seen by two women on my right, but not by a woman on my left! Then the sun was surrounded by brilliant coloured lights and appeared to be moving towards us eventually the sun set.

The next day it poured with rain. It was unlike anything we have here; it just deluged down and did not stop all day. We were all without exception soaked to the skin. There was no way to dry out. The houses do not have central heating or any other form of heating in the bedroom. One of our party gave her completely sodden fur lined raincoat to our hosts to dry out in the kitchen but it was returned just as wet, I would not like to go to Medjugorje in the winter. The trouble with material comforts is that the; are very difficult to do without especially as one gets older. After Mass the itinerary was to visit another visionary a young man of 23 called Ivan we went part of the way by minibus and the rest by foot through mud and blinding rain, Then again somehow I got pushed in with another American group and was within inches of Ivan .He answered the questions with a slight look of irritability on his face which was not surprising considering some of the inane remarks of the American matrons and the barrage of camera flashes. He too answered through an interpreter but appeared to understand some English. When asked if he was going to be a priest, said "That is private". After several questions he gave a lengthy discourse on young people. He said that too much freedom was given to children. It was then very difficult to get thorn to listen at 25. He spoke of the problems of drug addiction. It was obviously a subject he felt strongly about. The questions stopped and he then prayed giving an aura of great devotion and serenity. Soaking wet we made our way back to the minibus. We were not entirely surprised to find that had gone. Fortunately we got a taxi. After a short break we were to be taken to a neighbouring village where Father Jozo lived. He was the original priest at Medjugorje and had been imprisoned by the Communists for 18 months for his support of the children. This time a coach took us to his church. Most of us were still very wet .When we arrived a German pilgrimage was in the church and we waited until they left. Father Jozo had a friendly and leisurely way of speaking. He spoke at great length through an interpreter. The Yugoslavian and also the American priests all had powerful voices and gave incredibly long discourses, In England the congregation gets restless if a sermon lasts more than 20 minutes at least in my experience. Most of the Yugoslavians appeared tranquil and unhurried (not of course the taxi drivers) .The talk was very interesting and Father Jozo blessed us all and we took our leave. The rain had stopped a little and we were able to enjoy the Yugoslavian countryside. It was quite different from England, everywhere there were hills and mountains made of huge stoned and boulders. It is not arable land and the only crops are the grape vines and tobacco plants. Friday the feast of the Holy Rosary was a lovely warm sunny day. All our damp clothes soon dried out. .Surrounding the village are hills and mountains. On one of these hills Our Lady first appeared. Most pilgrims try to climb to the top some barefooted. It is extremely steep. We got the inevitable taxi to the bottom of the hill. An elderly nun, a crippled pilgrim and I tried to climb the hill. They both gave up and I managed to get to a cross about a third of the way up. There was a constant stream of pilgrims of all nationalities all with words of encouragement and a helping hand .Later during the pilgrimage we attempted to climb the mountain where they have the Stations of the Cross. We only reached the second station but we sat there peacefully and admired the superb view. The church with its twin steeples could be seen in the in the distance. Betty who walks with a stick had to be helped down by two young women, The climb frog top to bottom to top and back took at least 23 hours .Most of our party managed it. One young woman not from our party broke her leg near the top and they had to get her down by stretcher. At the top there is a large stone cross that can be seen for miles. On the Friday our hostess pointed to the cross. It was very dark but there were bright red lights round. The cross he watched it for some time. In the morning it was suggested that the cross was electrically lit, however pilgrims who went to the top said it was not wired for electricity. There are lightning conductors there. Anyway the following day I saw the cross lit at 3pm in bright sunshine. There are many supernatural signs at Medjugorje. Each evening at 5pm the rosary is said in the church. At 5.40pm Our Lady appears. Her arrival is preceded by three flashes of light in the ceiling. Unfortunately, his is also the signal for the start of a barrage of camera flashes. The priests request that the cameras stop. When the cameras flashing dies down it is then possible to see the supernatural flashes. These can last for at least 20 minutes and light up the church like searchlights. Ole night after a burst of what appeared to be lightning I saw a ball of blue and white light in the ceiling. The only way to get a seat in the church for the rosary is to get there an hour before. I felt extremely sorry for the local people. Their church has been completely taken over by visitors. The old Yugoslavian women dressed in black come into Mass and. there are no seats for them. The behaviour of some of the pilgrims is unfortunate An American priest admonished his congregation saying that it was a scandal the way the English speaking pilgrims talked loudly in church as they went out.

On the day of our departure the police moved all the gypsy stall holders. There is to be a wide road built so that the traffic can pass. We travelled back to Split along the beautiful Adriatic coastline and stopped for coffee in a lovely spot overlooking the sea. It was a fitting conclusion to our trip.

1988 Retirement: A New Life

I retired in 1988 after 22 years of service in the Civil Service. My office gave me a very good send off; my leaving cake was in the form of a swimming pool as they knew my favourite past time. Old friends came to say goodbye and I had the usual commendations from my bosses. It was quite sad in a way, but I was very tired and had enough. A VAT inspector's job was difficult; we were expected to go through all the books and agree the final accounts in just a few hours. In addition the travelling was traumatic at times; the only consolation being the mileage allowance. Although I had moved back to Head Office the area covered was extensive. John had retired a few years previous and found retirement hard, but he liked cooking, so there was always a meal waiting for me. This didn't continue when I was finally at home all day and he just cooked for himself as my cooking was pretty terrible. Our meal times were usually different as John liked the kitchen all to himself when cooking. He cultivated new interests including weekly whist drives and playing cards in the social club with new friends. He was a devout Catholic and attended Mass daily always sitting right at the back. Usually I sat at the front with friends. But John loved dancing and we attended the dances in the Club. New Year's Eve was always special, so we both entered a new social life which eventually came to an end when he died 8 years later after a long and painful illness of lung cancer. He had smoked most of his life from a small boy and gave up when diagnosed which in a way was a mistake as the harm had already been done and he enjoyed a smoke which might have helped the trauma of his illness.

I had to make many adjustments myself on retirement. Having spent most of my working life in (at the time) the male dominated Civil Service ministries, Home Office and H.M.Customs & Excise. I began an active interest in Women's Rights and by doing so had alienated myself from my bosses. I didn't find the Church very different in that the hierarchy were just as autocratic as the Heads of Departments in the Civil Service.

The parish priest when I retired was quite a character. He was a brilliant homilist although inclined to voice vehemently his antagonism against proposed alterations to structures in the Church suggested by the Bishop. A previous parish priest had left a great deal of money to the Church which the Bishop thought, according to Fr A, should be under his domain. This resulted in lengthy protestations in sermons and in the newsletters. He was a difficult man, but had many good qualities. Among them was a great love of children, the sick and the elderly. He took a great interest in ecumenism and started a local ecumenical group and also in promoting dialogue with the local Jewish Community. The money he received for the Church went to good causes, but he spent very little on the Church itself making do with old appliances and little on decorating and improving the structure. Also he spent little on himself or his curates. He had for a few years a bull terrier of uncertain temperament and the little mongrel called Heinz, who was allowed to roam the neighbourhood. He also had a large black cat that occasionally appeared on the altar during Mass. He enjoyed a drink in the social club and a chat with the regulars, but not the most regular Mass attendees. As my husband remarked he was a man's man - whatever that is. After a few drinks he would join the dancers in the hall doing his own version of an Irish jig, sometimes wearing a huge sombrero. Another pastime he enjoyed was a swim in the sea. Among his many interests were the Shrine of Our Lady of Lourdes and every year he acted as a brancadier (a volunteer helper for the sick, old and infirm at Lourdes). It was sad that unfortunately for such a brilliant intellectual man his memory started to fail, which he found hard to bear. For many years the Bishop had tried to move him to another parish but he refused to go. Finally he did suggest that he might move and the Bishop immediately transferred him to another parish, but his health rapidly deteriorated. I saw him go with mixed feelings; he had a cavalier approach to the laws of the Catholic Church given by their Magisterium. He was anti-authoritarian himself, but expected his parishioners not to challenge his point of view, particularly the females. As I had spent most of my working life enforcing governmental rules I found his approach disturbing. Finally I stopped going to Sunday Mass in order to escape his sermons. He told me once I was like King Canute sitting on his throne by the sea ordering the waves to go back. But I regularly attended weekly Mass. John and I had an active social life in the Church and we met Father A. frequently on amicable terms.

Soon after my retirement Fr A was moved to another parish and another priest was appointed. In his first Mass he told us that he hadn't wanted to move and didn't love his new parishioners. He was charming and charismatic, he liked women and they liked him, so in a short while he had devoted followers who worked hard in the Church. Like Fr A. he was interested in social justice, and set up a Justice and Peace Group. He also took an active interest in Ecumenism and asked me to take over the post of Minute Secretary in the local Churches Group. He also asked me to become a Eucharistic Minister and a Reader. With these new duties I became very busy. We worked well together, but I did have misgivings over his attitude sometimes, which led to heated arguments in Church. He was a kind and compassionate man but found his ministry difficult. Eventually he settled in and began, as he put it, to love his parishioners.

He spent a considerable amount of money on refurbishing the Priest's House and the Hall. They both needed a complete overhaul, but the Hall, in most people's opinion, should have been demolished in Fr A's time. Now over twenty years later a new Hall is to be built costing £1,000,000. Most of his sermons were on Love and Christ's Love and Mercy, but rarely on repentance. I said at our last conversation that he gave the impression that Christ was a weak and ineffectual man, whereas we believe he was a stern Father who rebuked his sinful children and insisted on repentance. After a few years he began to look troubled and was losing weight. He celebrated 30 years as a priest and the parish gave him a celebration party, but shortly afterwards he went on sabbatical; a period when a priest often reviews his vocation. We all hoped he would recover after a good rest, but he didn't return and we were not given any news of his whereabouts. It was a great shock to read in a Sunday newspaper of an affair with a married woman with six children, and that he was the father of two of her children. The parish was in a state of turmoil and disbelief not helped by the lack of information. Gossip freely circulated as it usually does, and the only news we had was from the newspapers. The Bishop came down to speak to us and in the meanwhile appointed a newly ordained priest to stand in. Eventually after due consideration by Rome he was allowed to remain a priest and posted to another area. It was all very sad and we prayed that he would settle down.

In the interim period while we waited for a new parish priest, the Bishop appointed a recently ordained priest to take over. He was helped by a retired Bishop living in the parish. The old Bishop had been greatly distressed by Fr B's behaviour, especially as they had been good friends, but Fr B. had not confided in him or anyone else. The new priest came, but I was regarded with suspicion as I had been friendly with Fr. B. It was also unpopular at Parish Council meetings as I usually queried the financial accounts. It was second nature to me to do so after years as a VAT inspector to question certain entries, but it was not my intention to doubt the integrity of those who had prepared them.

The first Parish Council meeting under the new priest went very badly as they sought retaliation with me. I, as usual, queried the accounts and later received a letter from the new parish priest suspending me from the Parish Council, my role as Eucharistic Minister and Reader. He hadn't had time to know anything about me so I realised he had been asked to act in this way. The parish was naturally very upset and so was John. As the PP was new and struggling to overcome all the resentment caused by Fr B's behaviour, I wrote back and said that I had been appointed by the Bishop to be a Eucharistic Minister and that I was the Ecumenical representative for the Parish, being the secretary of the main Churches Together group, and was re-elected annually. As there was no reply I decided the best thing was to ignore his letter completely, and went ahead with my duties. However I was upset and turned to the stand-in priest who had moved to another parish. It was a longish drive, but there was a good Catholic Bookshop in the area which I enjoyed visiting. The priest always made me very welcome and gave me tea.

He was academic and intelligent. My husband said he was a good protagonist for me. He was then made a parish priest in a more outlandish parish and entailed a longer journey. He was now working on his own. It must have been very lonely for him and he missed the close friendship he had with members of my parish. Our meetings became more social and he used to cook for me and take me to the supermarket when he did his shopping. I began to get uneasy as I went for spiritual direction and not a social visit also I realised that a lot of what I said was being relayed back to my parish. I was now on better terms with my new P.P. and I was worried about my husband's health so I decided not to go again. He was made a deputy spiritual leader of the Lourdes Pilgrimage and then the Leader. Unfortunately a fortnight before the Pilgrimage he had a prostate operation and his deafness was becoming more apparent. He was obviously upset and he described the operation to me and I sympathised but I kept him at some distance. The week went quickly and there were many beautiful services.

The Diocesan Pilgrimage always has a large number of young people who help to push the wheelchairs. By now I was in a wheelchair as the arthritis had attacked my hips. Lourdes caters well for the sick. It is always very crowded and getting on and off the planes can take some time with the disabled assisted on first. It is usually very chaotic and I was discussing the hold up when Fr C. boarded and he thought I was criticizing his leadership and snapped at me. Finally we were all seated. The lady next to me seemed to be ill and had difficulty in expressing herself to me or the air hostess. She didn't speak at all and I settled to a nice rest on the plane. In no time we arrived at Stanstead airport. Fr C. came up to speak to people behind me leaning on the arm of my chair. Unfortunately the plane had overshot the landing and we were told to fasten our seat belts as he taxied back. I hadn't undone mine so just I waited for the plane to stop. Fr C. then turned round facing me and leaning on my seat. Still feeling rather annoyed I stared out of the window and didn't look round.

Soon he started rubbing himself against me, but I didn't take any notice as I thought it was accidental. Then it went on and I realised it was deliberate –I could feel the dressings and his distinctive anatomy. The latter was the reason I knew I had not imagined it. It went on for sometime but I was too shocked to call out. Finally we were allowed to leave the plane and he rushed off to get his baggage and then he rushed away from the airport. Our coach was late arriving and I travelled back with some parishioners and two Anglican priests' recent converts to Catholicism. By this time I was very angry and spent the journey back moaning about priests without telling what had happened. Next day was a Sunday so I waited until Monday to see the retired priest as the P.P. was on holiday. The old Bishop gave the impression he had heard it all before and was more concerned when I said there had been a leakage from the confessional. I had discussed some parishioner's private lives and should never have been repeated. When I got back home I knew from their attitudes that they had been told what I said. Fr C. always denied this but I don't know how they got this information as I had told no one. As the old Bishop was not interested I wrote complaining to the present Bishop and was given an appointment at the Cathedral to see a senior cleric. I requested a hearing at a Church Tribunal but later I had a letter from the Bishop that he was not going to investigate further. Then I wrote to the Cardinal who wrote back to say the Bishop had absolute authority over his diocese. Then I wrote to the papal Nuncio who said the same thing. I consulted my solicitor but finally gave up. Later I felt I was left with a stigma as I wasn't given the chance to give my side of the episode. Thinking about it now, eleven years later I realise he was in a psychological state following so soon after his operation and his increasing deafness. My rejection of him as a priest and counsellor caused him to act in anger to humiliate me. A discussion might have helped to clear the matter up for both of us.

1988 Medjugorje – Second Trip

During Father B's stay in my parish a trip was organised in May to Medjugorje by a lady of neighbouring parish. Among the party going were a little group from London consisting of a woman with two sons, John (23) and David (21), and a nun. With me was my daughter, Hilary, who was 33 at the time. Opposite our room allocated to us were the mother and her sons. Hilary got friendly with the boys spending time climbing mountains. Hilary really liked Medjugorje and the trip to Father Jozo's monastery. Father Jozo is a charismatic healer and during prayers several people went up for his blessing (slain in the spirit). There were usually two men catching the people as they fell. It's a very unusual occurrence which I, along with Hilary, experienced. We were quite amused to see Father B fall on the floor. Father Jozo spoke through an interpreter and I believe he has never learnt English.

We stayed in a purpose-built hotel with waiters - quite unusual for Medjugorje. We had visiting visionaries giving talks. People of Medjugorje in these early days used to fast regularly – several times a week, mainly on Friday. Father B followed this strict rule of fasting and was often seen walking about with a roll of bread in his hand.

We enjoyed our stay in Medjugorje and on our return at Heathrow one of the boys, John, came up and asked my daughter to go out with him. I was rather surprised she said, "Yes", as he was ten years younger. By the end of the year they were talking about getting married. They Father B and he would not marry them because of the age difference, although they were both single and practising Catholics. They eventually married in the following March in a neighbouring church, which I found irritating as my church was next door, practically. However, it was a lovely wedding and my granddaughter was bridesmaid and we had a nice reception a local hotel.

The following March my daughter was pregnant and she and her husband went back to Medjugorje and Father Jozo blessed the unborn baby. Maria is 17, and like her mother, both belong to Opus Dei. They then went on to have three more children; two girls, and the youngest, a boy.

On a future trip, in 1994, I went with my friend, Zofia, and Christopher, my youngest son, drove us to Heathrow. On the way I said to my son that I would bring him and my husband back some Old Holborn tobacco. Christopher said not to bother bringing back Dad any, as he gave up smoking 6 months ago. And he has asked the family not to tell you to see how long it would be before you noticed. When we got to Medjugorje the war in Bosnia was on. We were greeted in Split by soldiers at the check-in. Our luggage was thoroughly examined and they were definitely hostile. We got on the coach to Medjugorje and on the way were stopped several times by police roadblocks. The Serbian police resented foreigners coming into Medjugorje, and they showed it!

At out lodgings there was a nice little group among them a young Irish brother and sister. I attempted to climb a hill called Podro. On the way down I had difficulties due to arthritis in both my hips. The young sister looked at me and asked her brother to assist me. He took my arm and I chatted with him. I asked him if he was a student as looked so young. He said he was a doctor. I asked if his sister was a student. She was a doctor too. They were children of a man in Ireland who did a lot work to help people in difficulties and homeless abroad. They had come over with medical supplies along wit another older Irish woman doctor. We saw very little of them during our stay as they went searching for victims of the war.

When we were leaving we were asked by a nun if we could part with any of our clothes for the homeless. Zofia and I gave most of our clothes we have with us. It is the only time I've come back with an empty suitcase. On our journey back to Split was hazardous, as we had to take diversions to avoid the police roadblocks. While in Medjugorje we visited a monastery where the Serbs had taken over and they dug up all the graves and played football with the corpses' heads. They were very cruel to locals. We heard many harrowing tales. We pleased to get home.

When I got home I asked my husband why he gave up smoking. He didn't say very much, but it was the beginning of a period of illness due to lung cancer. He had smoked for 60-odd years, and in a way, when he was diagnosed, it was a pity that he had given up. The damage had been done, he was terminally ill, and he would have enjoyed a smoke.

I went back to Medjugorje several times after, probably for the last time in October 2007, as I cannot leave my dog, Dougal. Of course, now there is now a beautiful new road from Split to Medjugorje. The villagers now have fax and computers and can be contacted by email. However, they are still very much country people. And where Christopher and I stayed they kept pigs, so we had plenty of pork and home-grown vegetables. There were about 30 Croatian men and a few wives staying there who were ex-soldiers and were very jolly; liked a drink and a smoke. They didn't speak English, but my son related to them very well, as Croatia was playing England that week, and they knew all the English players.

1995-1996 - John

It was in 1995 that John began to experience breathing problems, bronchitis and chest infections. The doctor suggested investigations into the problem. Fluids from the lungs were withdrawn and subsequently one lung collapsed. He was admitted to hospital for tests. John hated hospital .He resented the young nurses attending to him. Fortunately a male nurse who had recently lost his wife to cancer began to care for him and took to shaving him every day as John objected to being shaved by the girls. He insisted to using a commode by the bed instead of a bed pan or bottle .He was not an easy patient to deal with. Mealtimes were another problem as he was a very fussy eater due to the lining of his stomach being weakened by privations while in the Desert Army. When the menus came round in the mornings I chose light meals for him, but if I was not there they brought along heavy unsuitable meals which he just left on his bedside table. I was not impressed by the treatment given to elderly patients. Another problem was his fear of darkness a result of his time spent in care. At home he always had a small light near his bed. When I visited at night I used to switch on a bedside, light but the nurses always turned it off. I spent as much time complaining about his treatment as he did. The only thing he did not complain about was the pain suffered. Once while I was sitting by his bed, two young nurses came to see to his bed and one leaned against it. He cried out in great pain. It subsequently was found by a doctor who asked him to stand by the bed that he couldn't stand on one leg, although he had never complained about the pain. He was sent for a scan which revealed a second tumour in the leg. He came home but had to attend the hospital seeing the cancer specialist. The doctor recommended radio therapy but confirmed it would not be a cure. John refused the treatment and had to sign a disclaimer. It was nearly Christmas and we knew it would be his last and all the family gathered together for a Christmas meal.

We all enjoyed the Christmas celebrations and his illness was not discussed. January went by, but in February, one night I woke to see a golden chalice on the door. I put the light on and found it was on a picture of Christ taken and enhanced from the Turin Shroud. John was not sleeping well and was sitting.

In the lounge I told him about the chalice and he said to write it down and draw a picture of it as I might forget in the morning and would think I had dreamt it – I was rather surprised as he was not impressed by physic phenomenal and I was troubled by its significance A few days later, it was Ash Wednesday, he became seriously ill with pneumonia and was admitted again to hospital. He was put in a side ward and barrier nursed and remained there until he died on the Sunday after Easter-the Feast of the Divine Mercy.

Those six weeks were a nightmare he was in too much pain to talk much and eventually went on a morphine drip Barriers were placed round the bed to stop him falling out. I stayed at the hospital all day and Christopher came in at night to sit by him. Our parish priest was very good and also visited during the day or at night and administered the Last Sacraments. John was fond of him and sometimes when he was hallucinating due to the morphine he would say Father John is at the door. One day I went in and found him lying on the floor naked in the foetus position. He had taken off the morphine drip, made his way to the bottom of the bed and then down to the floor. I was so angry I verbally attacked the nurses, who said they called in to see him regularly, but it must have taken him quite a long time to get out of bed. I went on complaining about his treatment and a social administrator came down to see me and then a doctor .In disgust I wrote a long letter of complaint. John never recovered and went into a coma.

One Sunday I was at 8-0 a.m. Mass acting as a Eucharist Minister ,feeling very depressed as shortly afterwards I was going in to the hospital and dreading seeing John who was dying , but suddenly I felt very happy and I couldn't understand why. I had nothing to be happy about. When I got home the phone rang and John had died during the Mass. I knew he was now at peace and his happiness had communicated itself to me. Funeral arrangements had to make and the family rallied round.

The Requiem Mass was beautiful; Father John gave a glowing tribute to John and quoted the words from his army discharge papers which spoke highly of his army service. My three sons and my son in law carried the coffin out of the Church. He had asked specifically for a cremation which was attended by all the family including the younger members. I remained calm and not distressed. However subsequently while on a visit to Lourdes in August I broke down when they sang one of the hymns I had chosen for the funeral–sobbing and crying and couldn't stop My arthritis had worsened and I was in a wheelchair sitting as is the custom right in front of the Altar with several priests con celebrating . There was no way I could leave as the wheelchair attendants were sitting at the back. It was distressing but my friends said it was a good thing for the grief to come out.

The following Christmas I went to Medjugorje on my own as I couldn't face a family celebration. It was bitterly cold there with temperatures 20 degrees below freezing point. It was always a feature in Medjugorje that the electricity supply regularly broke down and the water system also failed. However we were a happy group and the proprietor cooked special English Christmas dinner for us.

1988-2008 Lourdes

In 1988 I made my first parish pilgrimage to Lourdes. It wasn't too successful as the accommodation was cramped and we were put in a small room with a double bed. John complained to the manageress and asked for a room with twin beds. It was quite early in our marriage that we changed over to twin beds. John who was ten years older than me had always slept on his own and so had I. We were both set in our ways and resistant to change. The manageress who didn't speak much English was annoyed and muttered about the strange English married couples who wouldn't sleep together. However she changed us to a bigger room with two beds. We were lucky really as our friends were put in one room with their teenage daughters. It was a happy group and with them John discovered the night life, always a prominent part of Lourdes, by visiting a nearby hotel that catered mainly for the Irish visitors. I gave up on a hectic life style and used to go to bed early to prepare for the next day's programme. Although a religious man, John did not take to Lourdes. He was used to Banneaux, a little shrine in Belgium, which was not commercialised or crowded and where we stayed at a monastery. He likened the underground Basilica at Lourdes to Wembley Football Stadium.

John basically did not like travelling abroad. He had spent 7 years in the in a tank corps with the Desert Army and then part of occupational army through Europe. He was always the typical Englishman abroad and expected everyone to speak and understand English. When we went to Spain he used to paddle in the sea with his trouser legs rolled up and a coat on. He bought the Daily Telegraph every day and fell out with the manager of the bar as he wanted lime with his beer. They both got rather bad tempered. He never went again.

I continued to visit Lourdes without John for the next 28 years. I became disabled in the early 1990s. So with my later trips I began to appreciate the spirituality and comfort given to the pilgrims.

My most recent pilgrimage to Lourdes was in May 2008, the 150th anniversary of the apparitions, with a group from my church led by the new parish priest. There were about 84 of us including children from the local Catholic primary school and their headmistress.

MY son Christopher accompanied me as my wheelchair pusher, a formidable task in Lourdes as the roads are narrow and crowded. When we arrived at Stanstead my son found that the tyres of my wheelchair needed pumping up. After searching we found the disabled help stand but surprisingly they had no pumps. So we boarded the plane, disabled going first, and we soon arrived at Tarbes airport, where the coaches were waiting to take us to our hotels. Their coaches have mechanical hoists to take the wheel chairs and their owners on to the plane, where they were strapped in. On our coach was a group of handicapped pilgrims. They were very cheerful and friendly and the leader offered to lend us a pump, and Chris arranged to go to their hotel to pick it up.

Among our group was a young man recently diagnosed with M.S. came in a motorised scooter escorted by his father. Chris and he became close friends. We were all smokers and as the French Hotels have a non smoking ban, we used to go outside to smoke . On two occasions elderly French men came up to us saying "Bon, it is good"

We had an extensive programme and visited many places of interest. Masses were said in various churches of historic significance including the Parish Church. We were fortunate

To have two retired priests in our party, one was 91 . He climbed the steep narrow, hilly streets sometimes in the pouring rain and then con celebrated Mass. One church I always enjoy visiting is the Poor Clares. It is very simple and without the ornate décor of many French churches.

Lourdes was very crowded and we stayed at a small hotel in a back street up a small hill.

Wherever you go in Lourdes you end up climbing a hill. However it was much quieter at night than some other hotels I have stayed at, where the pilgrims stay up until the early hours singing hymns. When I took my granddaughter, who was 14 , with me one year she used to visit the Grotto at night with friends while I anxiously waited for her return.

The noise in Lourdes is so great that they have recorded messages relayed by loudspeakers.

asking the pilgrims at the Grotto to respect the silence

Of course the main message of Lourdes is the healing of the sick, physically, mentally and spiritually .There are special lanes set out for wheelchairs and stretchers. On occasions when I was pushed by my grandson Daniel he invariably overtook on the lanes at great speed. There is a large hospital in the Domain and every night there is a torchlight procession where the various groups from all countries walk with their own colourful

Banners and sing in their own languages.

Among the places we visited was Bartres, a small village where Bernadette was sent as a small baby to be wet nursed by an aunt as her mother was ill. Another visit was to Boly Mill where she was born and where her father worked as a miller, then on to the small used prison where they were forced to live after her father lost his job.

Our priests said Mass in the Parish Church and afterwards we had tea and cream cakes in a local café. It was a beautiful day and we all relaxed in the sunshine.

It was time to leave and the coach took us to the airport which has grown considerably through the years. There we found we couldn't take bottles onto the plane which left some people drinking their Holy Water outside the building.

The journey home was quite short and we arrived home to meet our friends and families

Waiting outside the Church

SOCIAL ISSUES

I have for some years written up a magazine for the church including mostly social issues and ecumenical news which are too lengthy for the weekly newsletter.

One I have been actively involved in is Jubilee Action who work on issues relating to the abuse of children and the persecution of Christians in Muslim countries. Jubilee Action invites the churches to pray for those afflicted and give any help when possible. A recent initiative called 'Kids Behind Bars', of which I was sent a briefing paper, reports that children in the World's prisons are caught up in an international blind spot. Jubilee Action's sister organisation, Jubilee Campaign, is calling for a UN Rapporteur to apply greater pressure to the 192 signatories of the UN's Convention on the Rights of the Child.

The report states that the Democratic Republic of Congo is the 3rd largest country in Africa and the most heavily populated. Two thirds of the population of DRC is under the age of 25. UNICEF estimates that in broad terms about 30,000 children are under arms and comprise 10% of the armed groups. In the capital, Kinshasa, it is estimated that there are now some 20,000 children, on the streets. In the Philippines children as young as 9 have been found to have been tried in Filipino courts and sent to adult jails. Conservative estimates indicate that the population of child prisoners there has risen to 20,000, or 10% of the total prison population. For instance, one child named Edwin, aged 12, was arrested for stealing a pair of flip flops and was sent to an adult prison where he has been for 4 months.

For the purposes of the report...

- The term "child" refers to any person under 18.
- "Youth" refers to anyone within the ages of 12 and 21.
- "Deprivation of liberty" is the imposed restriction on the movement and association of an individual in a custodial setting by order of any judiciary, administration or other public authority.

Jubilee Action is part of the global campaign for children in conflict with the law, initiated by the Defence for Children Internationally (DVI).

Their aims are...

- To put no children under the age of 15 in prison.
- Use appropriate and therapeutic alternatives to prison.
- Focus on prevention.
- Improve the situation for children in closed situations.

Jubilee Action also works in Mumbai (formerly Bombay), India. Jubilee Action has two rescue homes in Mumbai. Kampatipura is the commercial sex district, consisting of 40 streets lined with brothels. Around 40,000 women live there with their children. Their demand for children to work in this industry is growing at an alarming rate due to the mistaken belief that children have fewer chances of contracting HIV, as the majority are born with the virus due to their mothers. Similarly there is the myth that a man can rid himself of sexually transmitted diseases if he sleeps with a virgin. 9 out of every 10 girls rescued from the Mumbai brothels are HIV positive. The aim of Jubilee Action is to prevent and protect every orphan of commercial sex workers from entering prostitution in Kampatipura.

Jubilee Action send me their news letter monthly which I include in the Grapevine a Deanery magazine

PORNOGRAPHY

Last year I received a very unpleasant email concerning chid hard core pornography involving children from 8 to 15 . After notifying the police and my MP David Amess I wrote it up in the Grapevine along with some statistics taken from an American organisation- Catholic Answers, as follows.

HOW TO FIGHT THE INTERNET PLAGUE

There are 4.2 million pornographic Web sites,with 420 million pages of pornographic material.

43% of all Internet users view porn sites while they are online

The estimate is that 72 million people visit porn sites each month

According to Media Metrix, more than 70% of men ages 18 to 34 visit a pornographic site each month.

2.3 billion pornographic e-mails are sent every year

According to research conducted by the London School of Economics

And Political Science, 9 out of 10 children from ages 8 and 16 have seen Internet pornography –usually without even intending to.

The Internet Filter Review reports that the average of a child when he is first exposed to Internet pornography is 11 years of age.

Of children 15 to 17 years old , 80% have multiple exposures to hard-core Internet pornography

In 1996 the United States Department of Justice stated

"Never before in the history of telecommunications media in the United States has so much indecent (and obscene) material been so easily accessible by so many minors in so many American homes with so few restrictions

These statistics refer to America but I realised it is a problem in this country as well when, I received the pornographic e- mail . Although there are several security checks on my computer unsuitable material (mainly indecent) is transmitted every day. It is easy for me to delete them but I do not want my grandchildren to see them accidently.

When I was a young girl The Catholic Church used to ban unsuitable books and newspapers, one of which was the News of the World. We used to tease my father as he liked the paper saying the racing pages were very good

It would be useless to ban any thing today but I am appalled at the near pornography material in some daytime viewing , and also the violence.

When I worked in the prison service pornographic material was not allowed to be sent to prisoners -----maybe it has changed now. They were not allowed to use bad language in their letters, now there is no restriction on swearing on the television. The f word was rarely heard, now even the women use it. Then we read every day of violence to children and by children and there seems to be nothing that can be done about it

When I can't get to Mass I watch a programme EWTN on Sky transmitted by the Catholic Global Television .They transmit a daily Mass from a Church in Alabama . The American priests are outspoken and in their sermons speak without reticence of the dangers of pornography and other social problems.

The American scandals of paedophilia in the Church has probably led to a need for priests to speak openly of the dangers facing children from men who enter professions (consciously, or not) such as the church, teaching and social work, with the purpose of soliciting sexual favours.

I remember once saying to my oldest son who was thirteen, to be aware of a teacher who other mothers said was touching the children. He replied that if he touched him he would knock him down. I never spoke to him again on such matters as living in a tough, poor working class area the boys acquired good knowledge of such problems. The girls were more sheltered and it was rare to hear of young female violence. Paul was and is a dominant male who fiercely defends his own rights. In today's climate he would probably be censured for hitting a teacher and I would be blamed as well.

Family Tree

ADAMS

John Harold Adams Born 1917 Died 1996

Company Secretary

DANIELS

John George	b.1836 d.1879	m. Emma		Master Miller
Offspring	Thomas	William	Samuel	
William John	b.1859 d.	M .Minnie		Carpenter
Offspring	John b1889	Nellie	William	Albert
	>John b1919			
	Ted b1942			
William James	b.1903 died 1981	m. 1927 Mary Winifred B.1900d.1960		Carpenter
Offspring	Barbara Rosemary b.1928	William Joseph b.1930 d.1970		
Barbara	b.1928	m. John Adams 1952		Civil Servant
Offspring Paul John b.1954	p. Anne	>Joe b.1984	>Danielle b.1986	
Hilary Mary Lucia b. 1956	m. John Rackham 1990	>Maria b.1991	Lucia b.1992	Francesca b1993
				Josephb. 1994
Nicholas Daniel b 1957	M. Meen 1995			

Christopher Michael b. 1959	M. Karen 1984	>Laura b. 1985	Bradley b. 1986	Daniel b. 1988
Bradley	p. Sophie	Lucia 2008		

ECUMENISM

Fr.B asked me at an early stage if I would take over the position of minute secretary to the local Churches Together. I accepted and remained committed to ecumenism for over twenty years first as minute secretary, then secretary and later to secretary to the overall main body. Due to ill health I resigned in 2009. Taking minutes can be laborious and time consuming . There were many meetings to attend, those for the general public and those of the executive. In the beginning it was a fairly novel idea for the churches to get to know one another and their ideology. For the main body we met in the local town hall, it was well attended with the mayor present, and coffee provided. It was always very cordial and I made several friends particularly in my local branch. For most of the time I used my own car for transport but the ministers would often give me a lift and in later years I relied on them

FR B attended most meetings and was well liked. He was charismatic and related well to people. He never attempted to impose the teachings of Catholicism particularly where there were divisions and several interfaith

Programmes were introduced. As he was popular in the church they were well attended by parishioners. On Sunday evenings we attended services in each others churches and these too were well attended. Christmas time the Borough Carol

Service was held in my church enhanced by the Salvation Army Band. It was quite a different world for me, as when I was young my church forbade attendance at another church. There was a problem for me in Communion Services as I did not take communion which puzzled people of different faith, but on the whole my beliefs were accepted. There were also Lent courses held in members houses. All these activities require a lot of work and planning, now they just have the Sunday services in summer

Another aspect was taking part in political events, this led to meetings with the MP. Paul Channon was our MP at the time and he was always courteous and helpful. Then when he retired I had to arrange a meeting for all the candidates and met David Amess. He became a good friend and helped my family on many occasions.

My friendship with Fr.B . was resented by certain individuals who made some slanderous assertions, which they repeated to the new parish priests

There is a tendency sometimes in Catholic communities for a minority

to show very un Christian behaviour. The next parish priest was influenced for a while until he realised the truth, then he became friendly and took an active part in Ecumenism. He again was liked as he was a quiet unassuming man and didn't impose his views at meetings. He made close friends of a Methodist couple, both ministers, and entertained them and others in his house. He became the chairman of the main body and relied on me to deal with correspondence and matters he did not have time for. In the dark winter nights he called to my house to collect me for meetings. He was very considerate and was used to escorting our elderly retired Bishop and realised the problems the disabled have getting in and out of cars.

Today Roman Catholic priests have little time to spare outside their parochial duties.

When he stepped down after the appointed time I resigned as secretary but continued with the local group. The shortage of priests and also those ministers of other religions led to a decline in ecumenical activities.

Our new priest who was working on his own did not take an active part in these meetings but accepted my participation in ecumenical work.

Nowadays the barriers and divisions between faiths has diminished

and in this country churches respect one another's beliefs. In latter years probably due to a shortage of ministers, there has been a rise in free churches and in house churches and they now dominate the ecumenical groups in my area anyway. They are mainly dedicated Christians with enthusiasm and persistence. The only problem I find is that without a hierarchy, they rely on very strong leaders, and they can be difficult to replace.

With the shortage of priests in my church it seems a good time to appoint women deaconesses. A male deacon can be married and perform many duties of the priests and there seems no reason why women are not allowed to follow a similar pattern. We had in the past many nuns who were excellent with children and families and now with the shortage of nuns they need to be replaced. Women deaconesses whether single or married can undertake these duties remaining in their own homes but obeying the laws of the church.

Although I have had some bad experiences I remain a devout Roman Catholic. Priests are men and they have weaknesses and failures as other men. However on the whole most priests I have met have been dedicated to helping people and are on call 24 hours a day. It is a lonely life and they face old age without the financial security a profession gives. The haven that used to be available has gone with the shortage of nuns and the closure of many convents. Now many priests work in parishes subject to their health, as assistants ,in their seventies, eighties and nineties. It is not a profession to be undertaken lightly .

My dog Lenny

My little dog died in January 2009. He had been my constant companion for twelve years. He had been blind nearly a year and finally his legs gave up.

Then I resolved not to have another dog as it could not replace Dougall.

However I missed a dog about the house, and his warm greeting when I returned from shopping. He was also a good house dog and barked at strangers which was reassuring at night. There were several burglaries near me which made me nervous. One day I saw an Advert in our local paper advertising for homes for homeless dogs, and telephoned them explaining that I couldn't walk a dog due to my disabilities. There was she said a lame dog with a spinal deformity from birth, which might suit me. Daniel my grandson drove me over to the kennels and we were shown the dog. We both liked the little dog, said be about two and had been in the kennels about a year. He was very pleased to see us and after preliminaries we took him home. Daniel said he would care for him if anything happened to me.

He hadn't been house trained and even now, if he gets very excited he cannot control his bowel but it might be due to his weak back legs. At first he was very restricted in his movements but as his legs get stronger he can now jump on a chair near the window and talks to the passer-bys.

He is an affectionate, good tempered dog and good company. His name was Lenny in the kennels which we have kept. His mother was a Jack Russell but his father unknown. However he looks like a fox and has its characteristics

He prances when he is playing he is very nervous and backs away at the slightest noise. Also he plays with the foxes in my garden at night. One night after managing to get him in, he started to bark at the window in the front of the house, then I heard a vixen moaning outside who must have followed him . She might have recognised his paternity.

He chews up anything he can find and I have to be careful when the postman calls. My little great grand daughter loves playing with him and kicks her legs in her pushchair which makes him retreat but soon returns.

He is also quick to pick up her dummy when she throws it in the floor which he then chews. He found my Age Concern device to call for help, on the floor, one day and chewed it. Fortunately It still works.

Life is more hectic now and I am hoping he will grow out of his worst habits, but even if he doesn't there is no way I would part with him.

Family Pictures

My 80th birthday—Jean, David Amess M.P. Barbara

John

Chris, Paul, Nick

Joe & Danielle

Chris

Dan

Lucia R., Lucia A. Jake, Laura

Hilary, Laura

Chris, Bradley, Lucia

Lenny

MY ILLNESSES

My health remained fairly good after settling down with the family and after retiring I spent most of my time taking part in Church activities. In 1988 I began to have problems with my left leg making sitting and walking difficult . When I went to Lourdes in a parish pilgrimage I had to have assistance and on one occasion FR B. pushed me in a wheelchair in the grotto. As anyone who has visited Lourdes will know, there is a steep incline on the way out of the Grotto and I am overweight so I felt quite sorry for him.

However I managed quite well at home as I was still driving. John's illness then began to preoccupy me. When he went into hospital I applied for a disabled sticker for my car which enabled me to drive there and back. Once John died in 1996 I knew I must get some urgent treatment for my leg which had got steadily worse. At this time there was large backlog of orthopaedic cases waiting for operations which could be over 2 years.

In September 1998 I saw my doctor who had on previous visits told me that I had osteoarthritis in my legs. .He then wrote to the hospital requesting X Rays . After waiting for an appointment I saw a rheumatologist in January 1999 who subsequently wrote to tell me that the X Rays showed advanced arthritic changes in both hips particularly the leg. and recommended surgery. Then I was given a date 1st July 1999, which they altered to 20th July to see the surgeon but I was booked to go to Lourdes on the 25th July so I asked for another date. Eventually I saw the surgeon on the 4th October and put on the waiting list for an operation. By 2000 I hadn't heard from the hospital and in March I wrote to my MP who wrote to the hospital. He received a letter back saying the consultant had prioritised the need as "soon" This apparently meant a possible 12 months wait . I it had been prioritised as "urgent "there would be a 6 months wait. He also said I should consult my GP   and ask him to contact the consultant if he considered I needed urgent treatment. I saw my doctor on April 4th and he wrote to the consultant on May requesting that my admission for surgery be expedited as my symptoms were much worst and that recent X Rays showed severe osteoarthritis in both hips. This was putting a strain on my hands which were also arthritic. .He also recommended that the operation be done under local spinal anaesthesia as I was very over weight- this proved a Godsend. I was then given an admission date of 24th July . Once again it coincided with my booking to Lourdes on 23rd July with my granddaughter which I cancelled. The operation went well although it was a strange experience as I could hear the surgeons cutting through the bone.

After a week in hospital discharged myself and went home in an ambulance.

My son Christopher was not expecting me and when I arrived home he was in the middle of laying a new carpet in the front room. Post operative care after a hip operation required very little movement, I was not supposed to bend down or lift anything. The worst thing was having to lie on my back in bed at night. This I couldn't manage and ended up sleeping on a recliner armchair. I made a couple of visits to the physiology department in the hospital and then found the strain of trying to walk too much for my right leg. At this stage I thought it would be a good idea to press for a replacement of the right hip.

There were also problems with the church. The building is old and not built for wheelchairs, scooters, or Mums with prams Both the outer and inner doors are very heavy and it often means waiting outside until a passer by (often a non Catholic) lets me in. .With increasing numbers of elderly people, many of whom use electric vehicles the position could get worse.

Fr Dan did make provision for wheelchairs with spaces alongside the front aisles. It is helpful for the sick to be near the altar and for the priest to give communion On the many pilgrimages I have attended this procedure of having the sick in the front row is always observed. It is also a good concept for children and the young to be shown compassion for the sick.

Another problem facing the church or rather the parishioners is that our hall needs replacing and the there are plans to build a new hall, which will it is estimated cost a million pounds. The parishioners have rallied round and are engaged in money making projects. However taking into consideration the defects in the church building it would seem feasible also to undertake a refurbishment of the church which after all is the main life line for the parish, and be contented with a more modest parish hall.

Getting back to my operations on a post operative appointment I saw the consultant on 12th March 2001 and told him I was experiencing considerable pain in my other hip. He sent me for further X Rays on the hip and I was advised to ring the consultant's secretary to find out where I was on the waiting list. I rang on March 22nd but she didn't know and transferred me to the Admissions Office. They said the waiting list was now 18 months for routine cases and 9 months for urgent cases. In my case it would be about March 2002 before they would consider an operation. The X Rays went straight back in my file and were not examined. I complained pointing out I was in considerable pain in my hip and back and the secretary suggested I made an out patient appointment for reassessment and eventually I was given a date of 24th September. This was cancelled with no reason given and I was given a new date of October 26th with assessments on the 22nd October for heart, blood pressure, etc. I had the heart tests and arrived at the Orthopaedic department at 10-0a.m. At 12-0 I saw a nurse who tested a urine specimen and said I had a severe infection, but I said I had no symptoms and was prepared to give another specimen which she refused. Then she took my blood pressure and said it was 197/172 and told me to go to my doctor immediately and that I was not fit for surgery. I saw my doctor at 5-0pm who tested a urine specimen and said it was clear but sent it to the laboratory for further tests . I told him my BP readings and he said with those reading I should not be allowed to leave the hospital. He then took my blood pressure which was 140/80 and said I was fit for surgery. He phoned the hospital but the department was closed so he told me to phone them in the morning.

In the morning I rang about 9-0am and spoke to the sister who apologised and said the blood pressure machine was out of order. She said the operation date had been filled and gave me a new date of November 20th and November 12th for assessments. I arrived at the hospital just before 9-0 am.

At 10-45 I saw a nurse and pointed out my doctor had received a report from the hospital, and there was no suggestion of an infection. Then she took my blood pressure on a manual pump which was 140/100 which she said was a bit high but said it was probably due to white coat syndrome (my blood pressure goes up when I see a nurse or doctor) This was true and my daughter has the same problem . Then I had to have a blood test. It was full up and we were given several apologies. After that I made my way to the X Ray Department. It was now 12-0pm and the unit was absolutely full and the receptionist said there was an hour wait, as I was exhausted she suggested I came back another day which I did. Then as I got ready to g in for the operation the hospital rang to say it had been cancelled due to an emergency admission, and gave me another date of December 5th.

Eventually I had the operation on December 6th AS before I had an epidural in my spine and remained awake during surgery. The surgeon and anaesthetist were friendly and helpful. Then I was taken to a post operative ward. When the effects of the epidural wore off I was transferred to an orthopaedic ward. It was the same ward as before, a nice friendly ward.

In the next bed to me was an old lady of 89, who had a hip operation a week or so before me. Unfortunately she had lost her sight after the operation and was very frightened, she was also rather deaf. She had lost her husband in August whom she had nursed for 15 years. We got on very well as we were both born in Notting Hill and talked about the old days. After several requests she was given an appointment at the eye clinic the following Monday at 10-30am. She left the ward at 10-15 and in the mean time her nephew came to visit. She was not back by lunchtime so her visitors went to lunch. On their return, remembering the time my husband had been left in the corridor for sometime after a scan, I suggested he spoke to a nurse and eventually he was asked to go ever and bring his aunt back. They came back at gone 1-30pm, she was cold, frightened and crying. Apparently she was not seen until 12-30pm after she asked another patient for help. She was very hungry but was told it was too late to get a hot meal. Her nephew was very angry and went up to the canteen and bought her a hot meal. Subsequently he wrote four letters of complaint. She was given a further appointment at the eye clinic for the following Friday. The doctor came along later and told her she might be discharged but this was reversed later and she was told she would not be discharged until her eye improved.

The following day she had a pain in her side which she put down to getting so cold as the eye clinic was outside the main building. The irony of it all was that she had paid £5000 for the operation but it would have cost £7000 in a private clinic. According to as nurse the surgeon and theatre staff were paid extra for a private operation but not the ward staff. There was a terrific shortage of nurses, two mornings running while I was there were only two nurses on duty on the ward coping with bed pans, making beds, washing patients etc. After a week I was thoroughly fed up and asked to be discharged. The nurse said I must see a doctor but he was not available, so I said I was going anyway and phoned my son and asked him to collect me.

The doctor then arrived and said I was not fit for discharge as the wound was discharging but I insisted that I was leaving and they gave me some dressings. Sadly I said goodbye to my companion, her eye had begun to improve but her deafness made communication difficult.

Christopher arrived with my grandsons and they helped me get into an old van with suspension problems. They hoisted me into a seat, it wasn't ideal but I was thankful to be going home. The second hip operation was easier to cope with as I was familiar with the domestic routine. District nurses called in to dress the wound and the GP doctor visited. It became time for my post operative appointment and an ambulance came to collect me.

With hospital transport it appeared I was usually first to be picked up and last to l eave which could take some time as we drove through the streets.

There were the usual crowds at the orthopaedic department and I sat resigned to a long wait I was seen by the nurse in charge. The operation was successful but she pointed out I would never be able to walk without aids as I had arthritis in the spine. She showed the X Rays and said there was nothing the hospital could do to remedy this, but she made an appointment for a visit to the physiology department. This I attended several times and particularly enjoyed the swimming pool. In the meantime I resumed my church and ecumenical activities. At that time I was still driving but knew it was only a question of time before I gave up. When that did happen I bought myself a scooter and was able to make short journeys.

In the summer of 2003 I began to experience skin problems. At the swimming pool I noticed my skin was red and itchy which I put down to the chorine. The redness and itchiness continued and spread over my body.

Eventually I went to my doctor who prescribed various creams and anti histamines . However it didn't clear up and she recommended I saw a consultant at the hospital. As usual I had a long wait and then heard from the hospital in December 2003 and was given an appointment in February 2004.

The consultant examined me and said I had chronic eczema. He prescribed some steroid cream and a blood test. A visit to the hospital is a lengthy procedure. After waiting to see the consultant which depends on the number of people there, also the dermatology consultants are very thorough and will take time to investigate the causes of the disease, so no one minds the wait. Then the pharmacy can take over an hour to prepare the prescription .There is a system now for displaying in various departments when they are ready Then the blood test department is always very busy. This has a ticket system going up to a hundred. On one of my visits I was pleased to see a fairly low number only to find it was the beginning of the next 100. However there is a small canteen run by the WVS which sells a good selection of sandwiches, and mugs of coffee. There is also a stall selling, (in aid of charity) various little gifts, stationery and toys.

On my next visit the dermatologist told me that my blood sugar level was very high and to go back to my practice doctor. After tests my doctor said I had diabetes 11. My practice has a diabetic clinic which I now attend regularly. Once a year I have a retinagraphy examination to check diabetic problems. As my brother was blind due to diabetes, I am grateful for these examinations. Recently my surgery moved into a National Health Primary Trust building which is situated at the bottom of my road, which is a God send. They also have facilities for testing blood, which again I find very helpful.

It is now six years since my first visit to the Dermatology department, and I am still attending every so often. Eczema, which I understand is incurable, tends to flare up regularly, triggered in my case by heat, diet and stress.

It troubles me more than any other of my illnesses as it affects me during the night. In bed the heat begins to irritate my skin causing sleep problems. These affects are alleviated by anti histamines which can leave one feeling like a zombie in the morning. The doctor suggested two possible treatments, but they both involved several weeks treatment at another hospital some miles away. Since it already costs £10 to go by taxi to the local ,the cost would be exorbitant. There is an ambulance system taking several patients,

which can take a considerable time . One treatment was to establish those foods causing allergies. The other was light treatment which I suppose would alleviate the soreness and irritation for a period of time. There seems to be a relation between skin problems and my diabetes. If I indulge in cakes or anything sweet, the eczema flares up. and also if I miss a meal.

Since a young child I have regularly attended Daily Mass. As the Mass is at 9-15 on most days it can be a struggle to get there on time. Church as one gets older is not only a spiritual benefit, it is also a social event. One meets friends and exchange daily problems mainly health. In fact for the elderly one's social life consists of visits to the hospital, doctor, pharmacy, various clinics, and funerals. Our church used to have Monday lunches and an over 60's club, but it requires dedicated people to run these events and today younger women have to work, to provide a reasonable standard of life for their families. . We do have a St Vincent DePaul society who visit the house bound and have occasional social events. For years we had a social club which was very popular, but our church hall is now decrepit and from the outside is an eye sore with broken doors and peeling paint. Inside the heating has always been temperamental and unreliable. There are plans now to build a new £1,000,000 two tiered centre but with the credit crunch we have to raise a considerable amount of money before the work begins. This could take several years. In the meanwhile the social life of the parish has diminished greatly. The other week I went to a 90th birthday party in the hall and it was nice to see old friends and talk about the times we used to enjoy in the past. Now one can attend Mass and not know the people round us.

There is a coffee morning after the "children's Mass" on a Sunday, but it has been taken over by the children and is not suitable for a quiet chat. As a grandmother I know children today have plenty of scope to enjoy their friends socially. The problem is of course the teenagers who need a more sophisticated social life and in many cases a more spiritual awareness of the world and its problems.

Back to my illnesses--- the latest problem is carpel tunnel and arthritis in my right hand, caused possibly by the pressure on my thumb and first finger when I use my scooter. My doctor referred me to the Rheumatology department at the hospital who told me that an operation was advisable. As this involved cutting the wrist, it would make life untenable, since I rely on sticks to walk. Living on my own it would be difficult to manage with usual domestic jobs for the period of healing, about 6 weeks. This I explained to the nurse, who said there was steroid treatment but it was not always successful. She said it would be best to go home and then decide what to do. However I decided against the operation for the time being. She gave me a splint to wear at night, which did not help much and also irritated my skin. The right hand is becoming weaker with little strength so now I use my left hand on the computer. With these complications it seems a good time to complete this biography which I started about 25 years ago. There are few benefits in old age, health problems get worse not better. One should be wiser and overcome character weaknesses, but I am still quick tempered, impatient and intolerant.

So now I am finishing my biography with the hope that my children and grand children will appreciate and perhaps benefit from it